STEAMERS OF THE CLYDE

THE WHITE FUNNEL FLEET

1896.

ROYAL ROUTE.

Price 1d.

ROUND THE CLOCK

A DAY'S SAILING on the Magnificent New Royal Mail Saloon Steamer

"Lord of the Isles"

BUILT 1891.

GLASGOW to INVERARAY and BACK (228 Miles), the Finest and Cheapest Day's Sail in Britain.

From GLASGOW (BRIDGE WHARF) Daily AT 7-20 A.M.

Partick Wharf, 7-30 a.m.; Govan Wharf, 7-33 a.m.

TRAINS—CENTRAL, 8-45 a.m.; ST. ENOCH, 8-30 a.m.

RETURN FARES (Available for Season).

		Saloon	Fore-Saloon
GLASGOW to INVERARAY,		SALOON, 6/;	FORE-SALOON, 3/6
GREENOCK	,,	,, 5/6;	,, 3/
DUNOON,	,,	,, 4/6;	,, 3/
ROTHESAY,	,,	,, 4/;	,, 2/

For Fares to Intermediate Ports see Time Tables, Bills, &c.

Famed Loch Eck Tour—One-Day Coach Tour,

GLASGOW, 10/; GREENOCK, 10/; DUNOON, 9/.

Special Reduced Rates granted to English Tourists from Glasgow, Greenock, and Gourock, by Steamer to Inveraray and Loch Eck Tour, on presentation of Return Half of Railway Ticket.

Breakfasts, Luncheons, Dinners, and Teas served on board.

M. T. CLARK, 5 Oswald Street, Glasgow.

STEAMERS OF THE CLYDE

THE WHITE FUNNEL FLEET

Alistair Deayton

TEMPUS

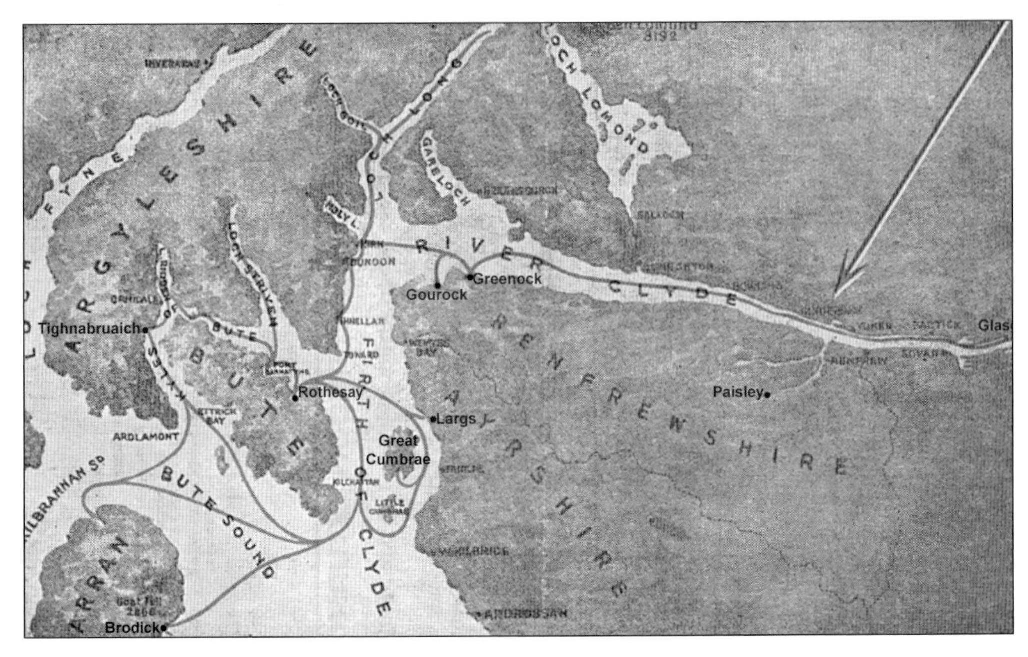

A map from the September 1934 Williamson-Buchanan timetable, with a note about viewing the New Cunard White Star liner, 534 (*Queen Mary*), being built at Clydebank.

Frontispiece: An 1896 booklet for *Lord of the Isles*. (CRSC Archive)

First published 2003

Tempus Publishing Limited
The Mill, Brimscombe Port,
Stroud, Gloucestershire, GL5 2QG

British Library Cataloguing in Publication Data.
A catalogue record for this book is available from the British Library.

ISBN 0 7524 2875 6
Typesetting and origination by Tempus Publishing Limited
Printed in Great Britain by Midway Colour Print, Wiltshire

Contents

Acknowledgements

My special thanks go to Archie McCallum, archivist of the Clyde River Steamer Club, for the loan of handbills and photographs.
Thanks also to:

Robin Boyd, for more from the CRSC collection
Tom Lee and C. J. Perrier for a couple of photographs from the Thames
The Mitchell Library, Glasgow, for photographs from the Graham Langmuir collection
Glasgow University Archives
Bruce Peter for use of photographs from the A. Ernest Glen collection
Robert Turner for an illustration of the former *Queen Alexandra* at Vancouver
Iain Quinn, to whom my thanks also go for checking the proofs and making helpful suggestions as to the location of certain photographs.
Douglas Brown

I have found the Java Perpetual Calendar on the internet:
http://my.execpc.com/~mikeber/calendar.html,
of immense value in putting dates to some of the 1930s handbills.

Introduction

Williamson-Buchanan Steamers was founded in 1919 by the merger of Buchanan Steamers Ltd (which dated back to 1852) with John Williamson & Co. (which had been running steamers since 1892). On 3 October 1935 Williamson-Buchanan Steamers Ltd was taken over by the London Midland & Scottish Railway, and the fleet continued to operate under the name of Williamson-Buchanan Steamers (1936) Ltd until 1943. Williamson-Buchanan Steamers and their predecessors concentrated almost entirely on the downriver services from the Broomielaw in the heart of Glasgow.

The Turbine Steamers Syndicate was a co-operative venture between John Williamson, the shipbuilders William Denny & Co., and the engine builders Parsons Marine Steam Turbine Co. to build the experimental turbine steamer *King Edward*. In 1902 Turbine Steamers Ltd was formed to operate *King Edward* and the first *Queen Alexandra* on the longer distance services to Inveraray and Campbeltown. In 1912 Turbine Steamers Ltd took over the Lochgoil & Inveraray Steamboat Co. Ltd, which had been their main competitor on the Inveraray run with *Lord of the Isles*, and which operated the Lochgoilhead service dating back to the dawn of Clyde steamer history. In 1935 Turbine Steamers Ltd was taken over by David MacBrayne Ltd and its two remaining steamers absorbed into the MacBrayne fleet.

Buchanan Steamers

William Buchanan was initially in partnership with Captain Alexander Williamson in 1853, owning the paddle steamer *Eagle*, first of the name. In 1862 she was sold for blockade-running in the American Civil War and, around that time, Captain Williamson withdrew from the partnership. Two other steamers, *Cardiff Castle* and *Petrel*, had been briefly owned in the 1850s. A second *Eagle* entered service in 1864 and she maintained the Glasgow to Rothesay service.

In 1874 Buchanan took over the Ardrossan to Arran service and the steamer *Rothesay Castle*. In 1878 she was replaced on this service by *Brodick Castle*, which maintained the route until 1886. In 1879, *Elaine* was purchased on the retirement of Captain Duncan Stewart and she continued on the Glasgow to Rothesay service, and the following year a new steamer, *Scotia*, was built for the Rothesay service.

In early 1885 seven steamers were taken over from Keith and Campbell: *Balmoral, Hero, Guinevere, Shandon, Vesta, Vivid* and *Benmore*. Routes to the Gareloch, Kilmun, and Arran from Glasgow – all operated by the former company – were all continued by Buchanan. Some of these new additions to the fleet did not last long, *Hero* being sold in 1886 and *Vesta* destroyed by fire at Ardnadam in the same year. *Benmore* was sold in 1891, *Guinevere* in 1892, *Balmoral* in 1893 and *Shandon* in 1894, at which time the second *Eagle* was also sold. *Scotia* was sold to the new Glasgow & South Western Railway (GSWR) fleet in 1891; *Elaine* went in 1899 and *Vivid* in 1902.

William Buchanan (Sr) died on 25 October 1890 and his three sons William, John and James carried on with the business, which was adversely affected by the new railway fleets of the Caledonian Steam Packet (CSP) and GSWR. In 1895, a limited company, Buchanan Steamers Ltd, was formed.

A new steamer, *Isle of Arran*, was built at Rutherglen in 1892, whilst *Guy Mannering* was purchased from the North British (NB) fleet in 1894 to replace *Eagle*, and renamed *Isle of Bute*. Another ex-NB steamer entered the fleet in 1904 to replace *Vivid*. This was *Duchess of York* (ex *Jeanie Deans*) which became *Isle of Cumbrae* in the Buchanan fleet.

The year 1910 saw the building of *Eagle III* and 1913 the purchase of the former CSP steamer *Madge Wildfire*, which became *Isle of Skye*. *Isle of Bute* was sold in 1912 and *Isle of Cumbrae* shortly after the formation of Williamson-Buchanan Steamers. The three operating steamers which passed to the new company were *Isle of Arran*, *Eagle III* and *Isle of Skye*.

John Williamson & Co.

When Alexander Williamson split from William Buchanan in 1862, he purchased *Sultan*, followed in 1868 by *Sultana* and in 1875 by *Viceroy*. In 1889 he took on *Marquis of Bute*. He retired in 1891 and sold these four steamers to the nascent GSWR fleet.

His son John Williamson purchased *Benmore* from Buchanan's in October 1891 and *Sultan* the following year, renaming the latter *Ardmore*. She was sold to David MacBrayne in 1894. A new steamer, *Glenmore*, was built in 1895, but was sold the following year for service in Siberia. *Sultana* was purchased from the GSWR in 1897 and *Strathmore* was built the same year to replace *Glenmore*. A sister of *Strathmore*, *Kylemore* was also built in 1897 but was sold on the stocks to owners in the south of England. *Sultana* was sold in 1899 and the small puffer-like *Alert* was purchased in 1900 to provide a cargo service to Rothesay. In spring 1908 *Strathmore* was sold to the Admiralty for service as a tender, and *Kylemore*, which had been running for the GSWR as *Vulcan*, replaced her. The final paddle steamer to be built for John Williamson was *Queen-Empress* in 1912. The Williamson part of Williamson-Buchanan in 1919 was thus *Benmore*, *Kylemore* and *Queen-Empress*.

Turbine Steamers Ltd

In 1897 the experimental craft *Turbinia* had, literally, run rings round the Royal Navy at the Diamond Jubilee Fleet Review, and Charles Parsons, the inventor of the marine steam turbine, was anxious to try the new engine in a commercial craft. In 1901 he, along with the shipbuilders William Denny & Sons of Dumbarton, joined with John Williamson to form the Turbine Steamers Syndicate and to build *King Edward*, the world's first steam turbine-powered passenger ship. She was designed along the lines of the CSP's *Duchess of Hamilton* of 1890 and the fitments could be seen along her deck where paddles were to be fitted if the machinery was not successful. The experiment was a success and the following year *King Edward* was joined by the first *Queen Alexandra*. The company Turbine Steamers Ltd was formed in 1902 and the two steamers offered day trips from the south bank railheads to Inveraray and Campbeltown.

In 1911 *Queen Alexandra* was seriously damaged by fire and was sold to the Canadian Pacific Railway, and replaced by a second steamer of the same name. In 1912 Turbine Steamers took over the two paddle steamers, *Lord of the Isles* and *Edinburgh Castle*, of the Lochgoil & Inveraray Steamboat Co. (their main opposition on the Inveraray run), and in 1914 the ageing paddle steamer, *Ivanhoe*. *Edinburgh Castle* was scrapped in November 1913 and *Ivanhoe* in September 1920.

King Edward and *Queen Alexandra* were requisitioned for trooping duties from 1915 to 1919. In 1927 *King Edward* was transferred to Williamson-Buchanan Steamers Ltd and a new turbine, *King George V*, appeared. She was an experimental vessel, fitted with high-pressure geared turbines. *Lord of the Isles* was scrapped after the 1928 season. In late 1935, *King George V* and *Queen Alexandra* were taken over by David MacBrayne Ltd, the former serving on the

Sacred Isle cruise from Oban to Staffa and Iona until 1974, and the latter, as *St Columba* and with a third funnel added, on the Ardrishaig mail service until 1958.

Williamson-Buchanan Steamers

John Williamson died in 1923 and his brother Alexander took his place. *Benmore* was scrapped in late 1920, *Isle of Skye* sold in 1927 and *Isle of Arran* in 1933. *King Edward* joined the upriver fleet in 1927 and a further turbine, *Queen Mary*, appeared in 1933. *Queen Mary* had the suffix *II* added to her name in 1935 at the request of the Cunard-White Star Line, to free the name for their Atlantic liner.

Following the sale to the LMSR in 1935, *Queen-Empress* was used on railway connection work and received a yellow and black funnel, but *Eagle III* and *Kylemore* continued on Glasgow services. All three were requisitioned as minesweepers in 1939 and *Kylemore* was sunk off Harwich on 21 August 1940. The other two were scrapped after war service. *King Edward* continued in service until 1951 and *Queen Mary II* received a new boiler in 1957, when her two funnels were reduced to a single one. She remained in service right into the days of Caledonian MacBrayne and was withdrawn after the 1977 summer season. She survives, moored in central London as a floating restaurant.

The Lochgoil & Inveraray Steamboat Co. Ltd

This company was formed in 1909 by the merger of the Lochgoil & Lochlong Steamboat Co. and the Glasgow & Inveraray Steamboat Co.

The former dated back to 1827 and had run a number of steamers over the years from Glasgow to Lochgoilhead, with coach connection to Inveraray. Towards the end of the nineteenth century these steamers were *Carrick Castle* of 1870 (which was sold to the Forth in 1881), *Windsor Castle* of 1875 (sold to Turkey in 1900), and *Edinburgh Castle* of 1879, noted for her exceptionally large paddle boxes.

The Inveraray company was formed in 1877 to operate the first *Lord of the Isles*, built in that year. She was a magnificent steamer and David MacBrayne was forced to build *Columba* in the following year to compete with her. She was sold to the Thames in 1891 and a second steamer of that name was built to replace her. After purchase by Turbine Steamers Ltd she was used for day excursions from Glasgow, mainly around Bute, until her demise in 1928.

The Glasgow & Inveraray Co. also operated the small paddle ferry *Fairy* from Inveraray to St Catherine's and the steamer *Fairy Queen* on Loch Eck. The Loch Eck Tour was a noted day excursion offering a steamer trip on *Lord of the Isles* from Greenock or Wemyss Bay up Loch Fyne to Inveraray and back to Strachur, a horse-drawn coach to the head of Loch Eck, *Fairy Queen* to Inverchapel at the foot of the loch, another coach to Kilmun or Dunoon and then a steamer home.

Liveries

Initially both Buchanan and Williamson used a black funnel with a thin white band. This had been inherited from the Glasgow Castles Steam Packet Co., and dated back to 1814. John Williamson changed to white with a black top in 1898, which was also used by the Turbine Steamers Syndicate and Turbine Steamers Ltd, and by Williamson-Buchanan after the 1919 merger. Williamson-Buchanan (1936) Ltd continued with the same colours, although *Queen Empress*, as mentioned above, received the CSP yellow and black funnel in 1938, when she was placed on railway connection service.

The Lochgoil company and the Inveraray company shared funnel colours of red with two white bands, a narrow black band between the white ones, and a black top. These colours were retained on *Lord of the Isles* and *Edinburgh Castle* after the takeover by Williamson. *Lord of the Isles* also had an unpainted copper waste steam pipe attached to each funnel.

One
Buchanan Steamers

In 1853 the Eagle Steamer Co. was formed by Captain William Buchanan, Captain Alexander Williamson and a gas-lighting manufacturer named John Cook. The company purchased *Eagle* on 12 April of that year. She had been built in 1852 by Alexander Denny at Dumbarton and was reportedly operated in the 1852 season by a consortium of various members of the Denny family and other Dumbarton businessmen. She had oscillating machinery by McNab & Clark of Greenock and was one of the first Clyde steamers to be fitted with feathering paddle floats. Williamson and Buchanan had previously commanded Clyde steamers owned by Denny's. The Eagle Steamer Co. operated her from Glasgow to Rothesay, the Kyles of Bute and Arran. (G.E. Langmuir collection, Mitchell Library)

In 1860 *Eagle* was reboilered and the two funnels were reduced to one. By this time Buchanan and Williamson were her sole owners. On 7 February 1862, Williamson sold his share to Buchanan and in October 1862 *Eagle* was sold for running the blockade to the Southern States during the American Civil War. She made one trip from Nassau to Wilmington and back, and three from Nassau to Charleston, and was captured returning from the last of these on 18 May 1863 when she was coming out of Charleston. She was sold by a prize court, but this was not the end of the story and her new owners put her back into blockade-running under the name of *Jeanette* and she made one trip from Havana to Galveston and back in January 1865. (G.E. Langmuir collection, Mitchell Library)

The Eagle Steamer Co. operated *Cardiff Castle* from 1855 until 1859. She had been built in 1844 for the Glasgow Castle Steam Packet Co. She is one of the two steamers with the black funnel with one white band on the far side of the river in this famous photograph of the Broomielaw. She was sold to Alexander Watson and Henry Sharp in 1859 and became notorious as a 'Sunday-breaker', sailing to Millport during the week. The trips of the Sunday-breakers were the booze cruises of the day; at that time public houses were forbidden to open on Sundays. Her ultimate fate is unknown.

Petrel, which had been built for the Railway Steamboat Co. in 1845 by Barr & McNab, was owned by the Eagle Steamer Co. from around 1853 to 1858, when she was sold for use as a 'Sunday-breaker'. Her full story is told in *Caledonian Steam Packet Company Ltd.*

In 1862 Williamson left the partnership to start up on his own account. A replacement for *Eagle* was ordered from Charles Connell & Co., but she was sold whilst on the stocks for blockade-running. This steamer was named *Mary Anne*. A replacement was quickly laid down at the same yard, fitted with double diagonal machinery by the Anchor Line, and this the second *Eagle* entered service in June 1864 on the Glasgow to Rothesay route. She is seen here at the Broomielaw in around 1865. In 1866 *Eagle* was lengthened by 16 feet, as her machinery was too powerful for her hull.

In 1876 *Eagle* was re-engined and reboilered, emerging with a single funnel. Her new engines were of the simple diagonal type, built by W. King & Co. of Glasgow. She is seen here in a postcard view at the Broomielaw.

In 1887 *Eagle* had a large deck saloon fitted aft on top of the raised quarterdeck. This was unique for a Clyde steamer. From that year until 1892 she operated from the Broomielaw to Brodick via Rothesay and Kilchattan Bay. From then until 1894 she sailed to Rothesay and was sold in that year for service on the then new Manchester Ship Canal. She was scrapped at Liverpool in 1896.

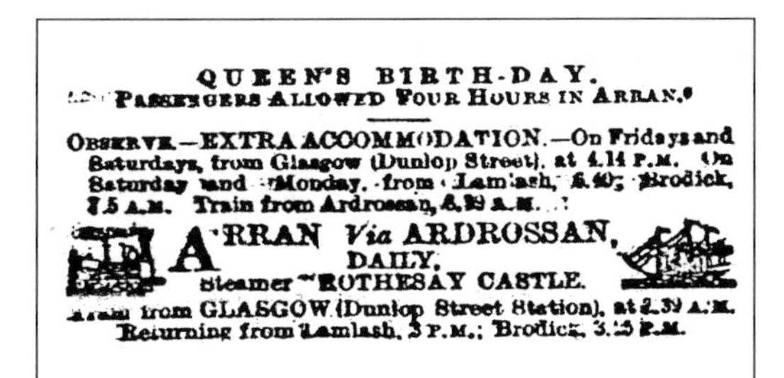

QUEEN'S BIRTH-DAY.
PASSENGERS ALLOWED FOUR HOURS IN ARRAN.

OBSERVE.—EXTRA ACCOMMODATION.—On Fridays and Saturdays, from Glasgow (Dunlop Street), at 4.14 P.M. On Saturday and Monday, from Lamlash, 6.40; Brodick, 7.5 A.M. Train from Ardrossan, 6.39 A.M.

ARRAN *Via* ARDROSSAN,
DAILY,
Steamer "ROTHESAY CASTLE.
Train from GLASGOW (Dunlop Street Station), at 2.39 A.M.
Returning from Lamlash, 3 P.M.; Brodick, 3.25 P.M.

An advert for *Rothesay Castle's* service to Arran for the Queen's Birthday Holiday in 1875. (G.E. Langmuir collection, Mitchell Library)

In 1874 William Buchanan took over the Ardrossan to Arran service from the trustees of the Duke of Hamilton. *Rothesay Castle* was put on this service. She had been built in 1865 by Henderson, Coulbourn & Co. of Renfrew with a steeple engine by J. McNab, and had been running on the Glasgow to Rothesay service since 1866 under the ownership of Buchanan. Replaced on the Arran route by *Brodick Castle* in 1878, she returned to it in the following winter and was sold to owners at Bordeaux in May 1879 and renamed *Gironde-Garonne*, in which condition she is seen here in this postcard view. Her eventual fate is unclear, but it is probable that she was scrapped around 1881. (CRSC slide collection)

In 1878, *Brodick Castle*, seen here leaving Brodick, was built for the Arran service by H. McIntyre of Paisley. She was fitted with the engines which had been removed from the second *Eagle* in 1876. She served the route until the end of the 1886 summer season, and was then sold to the Bournemouth, Swanage & Poole Steam Packet Co.

In 1894 *Brodick Castle* sailed for a season in the Bristol Channel under charter, firstly to the Bristol & Ilfracombe Pleasure Steamers Ltd and then, from 14 July, to Edwards, Robertson, after the former company had succumbed to fierce competition from the latter and from P. & A. Campbell.

After the 1895 season the Bournemouth, Swanage & Poole Steam Packet Co. became the Bournemouth & South Coast Steam Packets Ltd. In 1901 *Brodick Castle* was sold to Cosen's. During her period at Bournemouth she sailed from there to Swanage, Poole and other south coast ports, with the occasional special sailing as far as Brighton. In autumn 1909 she was sold to Argentina for use as a cattle-carrying barge. Stripped of her engines, boilers, funnels and passenger accommodation, and renamed *Ceca Nova*, she sank whilst on tow off Portland shortly after leaving Weymouth on her delivery voyage. (CRSC)

In 1879 *Elaine*, formerly owned by Captain Duncan Stewart, was taken over by Buchanan. She had been built for Graham Brymner & Co. in 1867 for the Glasgow to Millport service by R. Duncan & Co. of Port Glasgow with two-cylinder oscillating engines by Rankin & Blackmore. In 1874 Captain Duncan Stewart purchased her for the Glasgow to Rothesay route. He died at the end of 1877 and his two sons gave up steamer-owning in 1879. In August 1878 she was chartered to run from Ardrishaig and Skipness to Tarbert carrying voters for a by-election. On her return through the Kyles of Bute she ran aground and sank opposite Tighnabruiach. She was refloated, repaired and towed to Greenock for repairs. This illustration shows her in around 1885. (Douglas Brown collection)

Elaine at Carrick Castle, presumably on a special public holiday sailing or a charter. Note the bathers on the beach. She continued on the service from Glasgow to Rothesay and later to Lochgoilhead until the end of the 1899 season, when she was sold for breaking up at Bowling.

In 1880 *Scotia* was built by H. McIntyre of Paisley with a two-cylinder steeple engine by W. King & Co.; it was the last steeple engine, and the only two-cylinder one, to be built for a Clyde steamer. She was built for Buchanan's Glasgow to Rothesay service. In 1885 she moved to the Glasgow to Arran via the Kilchattan Bay route and in 1887 to the Ardrossan to Arran route. In July 1891 she was sold, along with the goodwill of the Ardrossan to Arran service, to the Glasgow & South Western Railway. Behind her here as she leaves the Broomielaw is *Vivid*, with the white Campbell funnel. For her later history see *Glasgow and South Western and Other Steamers*.

In 1885 William Buchanan took over the seven steamers of Keith & Campbell, which had been operating from Glasgow to Helensburgh, the Gareloch, Arran, and the Holy Loch. The veteran *Balmoral*, here leaving Dunoon, was the oldest of these. J. Barr of Paisley had built her in 1842, with a steeple engine by Barr & McNab, for the McKellar fleet, sailing from Glasgow to Largs and Millport as *Lady Brisbane*. In 1868 she passed into the fleet of Hugh Keith. On 18 April of that year she sank off Bowling after a collision with a tug. She was raised, refurbished, and renamed *Balmoral*. Placed on the Gareloch route, she remained on that service during Buchanan's ownership until her engines gave up the ghost in 1890 and she was sold for use as a coal hulk at Newry.

Hero had been built in 1858 by T. Wingate & Co., with a steeple engine by her builders. After a varied early career, she entered the fleet of Hugh Keith in 1878. He placed her on the Gareloch service, but when purchased by Buchanan, she was used by him as a spare boat and for relief sailings and charters. In 1886 she was sold to the River Tay Steamboat Co. and in April 1889 to a Mr Orr of Glasgow who ran her on excursions from Dumbarton and Paisley, and in 1890 she was sold to David MacBrayne. She became his second *Mountaineer* and operated on excursions from Oban until scrapped after the 1909 season. She is seen here as *Hero*, leaving Row (as Rhu was then spelt) with *Shandon* approaching in the distance. (From the CRSC magazine 1983)

Guinevere had been built in 1869 by R. Duncan & Co., with two-cylinder oscillating machinery by Rankin & Blackmore, for Graham Brymner & Co. for his service from Glasgow to Arran, landing passengers at Corrie, Brodick, Lamlash and Whiting Bay by ferry until the piers were completed at Brodick in 1872 and at Lamlash in 1884. She called en route at Kilchattan Bay in the south of Bute, where a pier was built in 1880. In 1869 she also called at Wemyss Bay and, from 1870, at both Greenock Princes Pier and Custom House Quay. Hugh Keith purchased her in November 1876. In 1880 she sailed on certain days to Skipness, Lochranza and Pirnmill, alternating with *Glen Rosa* on the east Arran route, but returned to the latter in 1881 after *Glen Rosa* left the river.

A W. Ralston & Co. view of *Guinevere*. She was replaced by *Scotia* on the Arran route and was moved to the Glasgow to Rothesay service after purchase by Buchanan in 1885. On 20 April 1891 she undertook an excursion from Paisley to Rothesay. She was sold to Turkish owners in 1892, but was lost with all hands during a storm in the Bay of Biscay on her delivery voyage.

Shandon had been built in 1864 by Blackwood & Gordon as *Chancellor* for the Loch Lomond Steamboat Co.'s service from Helensburgh to Arrochar. She came into the ownership of Keith & Campbell in April 1880 and was renamed *Shandon* for the Gareloch service. In both 1891 and 1893 she ran a single excursion from Paisley to the Gareloch.

In 1894, *Shandon* was sold for service on the Manchester Ship Canal and renamed *Daniel Adamson*. In 1896 she came back to the Clyde under that name for a short season and is seen here leaving the Broomielaw in a well-known photograph. Like the Loch Lomond steamers, she had sponsons that extended from bow to stern, which can be seen to advantage here. Also in this illustration are *Iona* in the middle of the river, *Benmore* berthed, and a number of Irish steamers to the right.

Vesta had been built in 1853 for J. Barr for Henderson & McKellar, running from Glasgow to Helensburgh. She came under the ownership of Captain Robert Campbell of Kilmun in 1866, running to Kilmun, and was the last flush-decked steamer to operate on that service. His fleet was merged with that of Hugh Keith in 1871, although this merger was a somewhat loose arrangement with both fleets keeping their old funnel colours, and in 1877 she was transferred to the Gareloch service. In March 1885 she was run over by one of the Clyde Navigation Trust's hopper barges off Greenock, and was run aground to avoid sinking. She was returned to service but, almost exactly a year later, she was destroyed by fire whilst lying at Ardnadam Pier. (Wotherspoon collection, Mitchell Library)

Vivid had been built by Barclay Curle in 1864 for Captain Bob Campbell for his service to Kilmun. She was sold for breaking up in the Pudzeoch at Renfrew in 1902, by which time she had the last steeple engine of any Clyde steamer. (Douglas Brown collection)

Benmore had been built by T.B. Seath at Rutherglen in 1876, with single-cylinder diagonal machinery by W. King & Co., for Captain Robert Campbell for the Glasgow and Greenock to Kilmun service, which included a weekly call at Lochgoilhead in her early years. She is seen here at the Broomielaw on Glasgow Fair Saturday 1885, still with Campbell's funnel colours, after being taken over by Buchanan. In mid-river is Campbell's *Meg Merrilies*, which he had purchased subsequent to selling his previous fleet to Buchanan. In the summer of 1885 Buchanan and Campbell were sailing in competition on the Kilmun service. Inboard of *Benmore* is *Eagle*, with *Vivid* in front of her and the then new *Chancellor* in the right foreground.

In 1886, *Benmore* was placed on the Rothesay service. In 1887 she was reboilered and a second funnel was added. (A. Ernest Glen collection)

Benmore in her two-funnelled condition. At the same time a small fore-saloon was added. The new set-up was not successful, causing her to be down by the head, and in 1888 she reverted to a single funnel.

Benmore around 1890. In that year she was again re-boilered. For a week in July she offered excursions from Ayr, Troon and Ardrossan, but in 1891 she reverted to the 11:00 sailing from Glasgow to Rothesay, with occasional excursions from Ayr. In October 1891 she was sold to Captain James Williamson. For details of her subsequent career see Chapter Two: Williamson Steamers. (Douglas Brown collection)

Above: In 1892 a new steamer, *Isle of Arran*, was built to replace *Eagle* on the Glasgow to Arran route, and she was launched by T.B. Seath for Buchanan Steamers. She was the first Buchanan steamer to have a steel hull, previous ones having being iron-hulled. Her single diagonal machinery came from W. King & Co. again. She was launched, as seen here, on 14 May 1892, and was the last Clyde steamer to be built at this yard. (CRSC)

Opposite below: A view of *Benmore* at the Broomielaw in a river-level view. From 1888 she made occasional sailings on the Ardrossan to Arran run to relieve *Scotia* when the latter was out of service. From 1889 she was used on a variety of excursions, e.g. from Helensburgh to Campbeltown via the Kyles and to Ayr and from Rothesay to Campbeltown via Brodick, Lamlash and Whiting Bay. (CRSC Archive)

Isle of Arran in Rothesy Bay in her first season. As can be seen she was a considerable improvement on previous steamers in the fleet with both fore and aft deck saloons. (Douglas Brown collection)

Isle of Arran leaving the Broomielaw in April 1894. *Madge Wildfire* is arriving upstream, probably on her morning up run from Kilmun. *Clutha No.10* is proceeding downstream and a Clyde Shipping Co. paddle tug can be seen alongside the cargo vessel with the black funnel with white band on the south bank, with another *Clutha* coming upstream ahead of her. (Annan Photographers)

SHIPPING.

EXCURSIONS Per ISLE OF ARRAN Daily.
Monds. & Thurs. to Loch Striven, calling Port-Bannatyne.
Tues. & Frids. to Loch Ridden, Do. Do.
Weds. & Sats. Round Cumbrae, calling Kilchattan Bay.

CHEAP DAILY EXCURSIONS Daily, from Bridge Wharf, calling at Intermediate Ports.

VIVID, 10 A.M.
ISLE OF ARRAN, 11 A.M.; Train, St Enoch, 12.5 P.M.
Leaving Rothesay at 2.30 and 4.45; Dunoon, 3.10 and 5.20 P.M.

		Steerage.	Saloon.
RETURN FARES:—	Dunoon......	1s	1s 6d
Do.	Rothesay......	1s 6d	2s
Do.	(Isle of Arran only), including Dinner and Tea, 4s 3d.		

An advertisement for excursions on *Isle of Arran* for 2 July 1894 from the *North British Daily Mail.*

After the 1893 season Buchanan gave up the Arran service and *Isle of Arran* moved to the Rothesay service, where she is seen here, with the CSP paddler *Duchess of Hamilton* at the other end of the pier. (Douglas McGowan collection)

Isle of Arran at the pier at Coulport on an evening cruise with the Glasgow Orpheus Choir. The awning which covered her promenade deck aft of the funnel can be seen to advantage in this view. (CRSC)

Isle of Arran leaving the Broomielaw on 22 May 1914. At the quay is *Lord of the Isles* with, aft of her, *Isle of Cumbrae* and *Isle of Skye*, with *Lady Rowena* in Cameron's colours almost up at the railway bridge. (From a CRSC calendar, W. Lind collection)

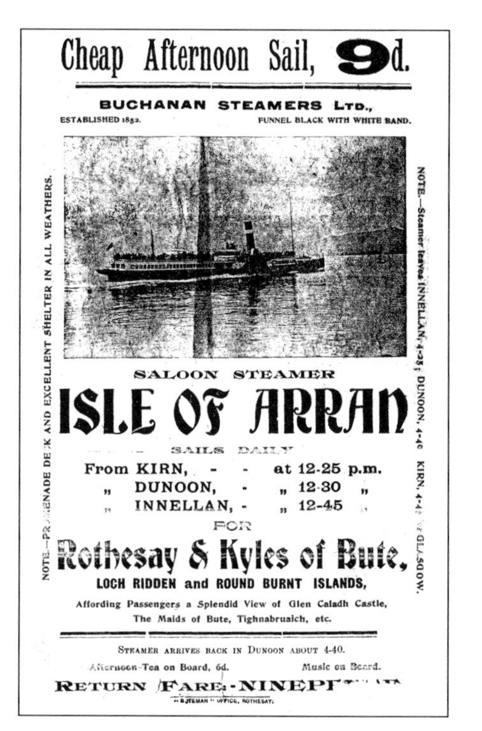

Above: An undated advertisement for *Isle of Arran* for excursions from Kirn, Dunoon and Innellan to the Kyles of Bute for only ninepence (less than 4p).

Right: Steamer advertisements from the *Evening Citizen* for 18 April 1913, including a sailing by *Isle of Arran* to see the launch of Cunard's *Aquitania* from John Brown's yard at Clydebank.

SUNDAY SAILING

Saloon Steamer

"ISLE OF ARRAN"

Sails from Bridge Wharf at 11 a.m., Govan 11.15, Bowling 12 Noon, Greenock (Princes Pier) 12.45 p.m., for DUNOON and ROTHESAY, thence on a CRUISE THROUGH THE KYLES OF BUTE.

Returning from Rothesay 4 p.m., Dunoon 4.40 p.m., for Greenock and Glasgow. Arriving in Glasgow about 7 p.m.

RETURN FARES.

	Saloon.	Steerage.
Dunoon	2/-	1/6
Rothesay	2/6	2/-
Kyles of Bute	3/6	2/6

Whole Day's Sail (Saloon), with Dinner and Plain Tea, 6/-.

BUCHANAN STEAMERS, LTD., 10 Bridge Wharf.

PASSENGERS by "ISLE OF SKYE" have a Splendid Opportunity of VIEWING the Huge Cunarder "AQUITANIA," at CLYDEBANK.

DAILY SAILINGS.

Saloon Steamer "ISLE OF SKYE".

Sails from BRIDGE WHARF at 11 a.m., GOVAN 11.15, RENFREW 11.30, BOWLING 12 Noon, GREENOCK 12.45 p.m., for KIRN, DUNOON, INNELLAN, and ROTHESAY.

Returning from Rothesay 4, Dunoon 4.40 p.m., arriving in Glasgow about 7 p.m.

LAUNCH OF "AQUITANIA,"

MONDAY, 21st APRIL.

Saloon Steamer

"ISLE OF ARRAN"

(Weather favourable)

Sails from BRIDGE WHARF at 11.30 a.m. for CLYDEBANK.

Returning immediately thereafter.

FARE, ONE SHILLING.

TO THE

LAUNCH OF THE "AQUITANIA."

The Magnificent Saloon Steamer

"LADY ROWENA"

Will Sail from BRIDGE WHARF at 11.30 a.m.

Calling GOVAN and RENFREW, for CLYDEBANK, affording Passengers a Splendid View of the LAUNCH. Returning to RENFREW, GOVAN, and GLASGOW immediately thereafter.

RETURN FARE, 1/-

Luncheon served on board, 1s 6d.

"LADY ROWENA" S. P. CO., LTD., 8 BRIDGE WHARF.

LAUNCH OF THE

"AQUITANIA,"

Steamers from Glasgow (Bridge Wharf) to view the Launch will Sail as under:—

(Weather Favourable)

"QUEEN ALEXANDRA" ...... at 11.30 a.m.

"KYLEMORE" .... at 11.45 a.m.

Also (if required),

"QUEEN-EMPRESS" .... at 11.45 a.m.

Steamers return to Glasgow immediately after the Launch.

Fare, per "Queen Alexandra" .... 1s 6d.

Fare, per "Kylemore" or "Queen-Empress"... 1s 0d.

Tickets can now be had from JOHN WILLIAMSON, 99 Great Clyde St., Glasgow.

SUNDAY SAILINGS.

Saloon Steamer, "ISLE OF ARRAN" or "EAGLE III."

Sails every Sunday (during Season) from Bridge Wharf, GLASGOW, at 11 a.m; GOVAN, 11.10; BOWLING, 12 noon; GREENOCK (Princes Pier), 12.45 p.m., for DUNOON, ROTHESAY, and Cruise through the KYLES OF BUTE. Returning from Rothesay, 4.45 p.m.; Dunoon, 5.25 p.m.; arriving in Glasgow about 7.45 p.m.

RETURN FARES:

DUNOON,	Steerage,	1/6	Saloon,	2/-
ROTHESAY,	„	2/-	„	2/6
KYLES OF BUTE,	„	2/6	„	3/6

Whole Day's Sail with Dinner and Plain Tea, 6/-

NOTE.—Only Temperance Refreshments Sold on Sundays.

SEE DAILY NEWSPAPERS FOR ALTERATIONS.

SPECIAL NOTICE TO PASSENGERS. We desire to call the attention of Passengers to the advantage of taking the 4/6 Ticket for the Week Days' Outing with Meals included. Sold only on board the 9.20, 10, and 11 a.m. Steamers. The value is unequalled anywhere. Give it a Trial.

BUCHANAN STEAMERS, Ltd.

OFFICE: 10 BRIDGE WHARF, GLASGOW.
TELEPHONE: 326 ARGYLE.

Left: An undated (1910-1914) advertisement for Sunday cruises on *Isle of Arran* or *Eagle III* to the Kyles of Bute. Note the line, 'Only Temperance Refreshment sold on Sundays' – Buchanan's were obviously anxious to distance themselves from the previous bad reputation of 'Sunday-breakers'. The Sunday service had started in 1903.

SPECIAL NOTICE TO PASSENGERS.

WE desire to call the attention of Passengers to the advantage of taking the 4/6 Ticket for the Day's Outing with Meals included. Sold only on board the 10 and 11 a.m. Steamers.

The value is unequalled anywhere. Give it a trial.

BUCHANAN STEAMERS, Ltd.

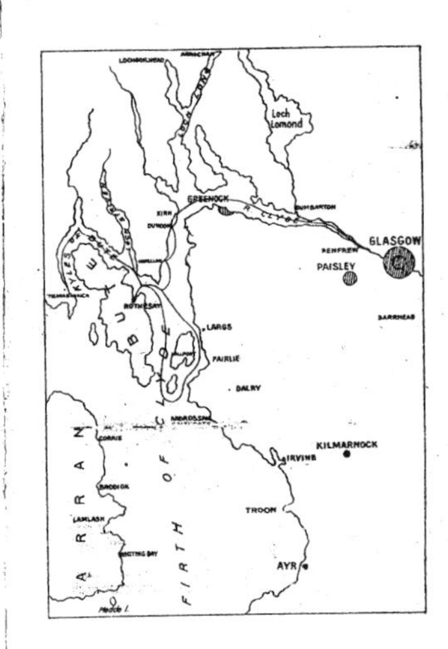

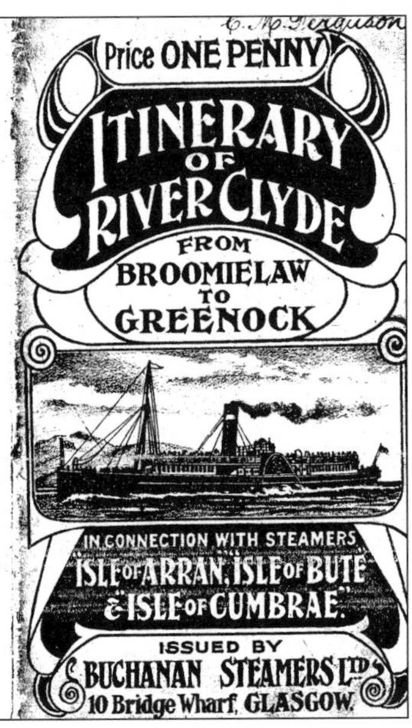

The cover of a descriptive brochure of the journey down the Clyde, featuring *Isle of Arran*.

DAILY PLEASURE SAILINGS

– TO –

Kirn, Dunoon, Innellan, and Rothesay.

Saloon Steamers Sail from Bridge Wharf,

"ISLE OF BUTE," 10 a.m.

"ISLE OF ARRAN," 11 a.m.

Returning in the Evening.

RETURN TICKETS:

	Steerage.	Saloon.
DUNOON,	- X 1/-	X 1/6
ROTHESAY, -	1/6	2/-

Day's Sail (Including Dinner and Plain Tea), 4/6

Tickets available during Season by either Steamer.
Week-day Tickets not available on Sundays.

X NO RETURN TICKETS ISSUED TO DUNOON DURING HOLIDAYS.

For further particulars, see Daily Newspapers.

Sunday Sailings.

Saloon Steamer "ISLE OF ARRAN"
(Or "Isle of Bute"),

Sails every SUNDAY (during Season) from BRIDGE WHARF, GLASGOW, at 11 a.m.; GOVAN, 11.10; BOWLING, 12 noon, for GREENOCK (Princes Pier), DUNOON, ROTHESAY, and Cruise through the KYLES OF BUTE. Returning from ROTHESAY, 4.45 p.m.; DUNOON, 5.25 p.m.; Arriving in GLASGOW about 7.45 p.m.

RETURN FARES:

DUNOON, - -	Steerage, 2/-;	Saloon, 3/-
ROTHESAY, -	„ 2/6;	„ 3/6
KYLES OF BUTE,	„ 3/-;	„ 4/-

Whole Day's Sail with Dinner and Plain Tea, 6/6.

Sunday Afternoon Cruise
TO
DUNOON and LOCH LONG.

Saloon Steamer "ISLE OF CUMBRAE"
(Or "Isle of Bute"),

Sails every SUNDAY (during Season) from BRIDGE WHARF, GLASGOW, at 2 p.m.; GOVAN, 2.10; BOWLING, 3 p.m., for PRINCES PIER and DUNOON, thence on a Cruise to ARDGOIL, Glasgow's Highland Estate. Returning from Dunoon at 6 p.m. (Dunoon passengers will have about 2 hours on shore), arriving in Glasgow about 8.20 p.m.

RETURN FARES:

GREENOCK, -	Steerage, 1/3;	Saloon, 1/9
DUNOON, - -	„ 1/6;	„ 2/-
CRUISE, - -	„ 2/-;	„ 3/-
CRUISE (with High Tea),	—	„ 4/-

NOTE:—Only Temperance Liquors Sold on Sundays.

Popular Excursions.

From 1st May to 30th Sept.
Saloon Steamer
"ISLE OF ARRAN"
Daily from Bridge Wharf at 11 a.m.

Mondays and Thursdays, -	To Loch Striven.
Tuesdays and Fridays, -	To Kyles of Bute.
Wednesdays and Saturdays, -	Round Island of Cumbrae.

Arriving in Glasgow about 7.45 p.m.

RETURN FARES:

Steerage 2/-. Saloon 2/6.

Whole Day's Sail with Dinner and Plain Tea, 4/6.

DURING JULY AND AUGUST.

UP THE KYLES OF BUTE

Daily, by Steamer
"ISLE OF BUTE"
From Bridge Wharf, Glasgow, at 10 a.m.
Arriving Back about 7 p.m.

FARES:

Saloon 2/6. Steerage 2/-.

Whole Day's Sail with Dinner and Plain Tea, 4/6.

Details of sailings from the previous brochure, which dates from between 1904 (when *Isle of Cumbrae* was purchased) and 1911 (after which *Isle of Bute* was sold).

Isle of Arran at the Broomielaw, with *Ivanhoe* under way alongside her. From 1917 to 1920 she was requisitioned for use as as a minesweeper and troop transport.

In 1920, when she came back from war service, *Isle of Arran* came into the Williamson-Buchanan fleet, and received their funnel colours of white with black top. Her bridge was moved forward of the funnel and the forward landing platform on the sponsons was plated in. She is seen here, well filled, off Dunoon. The small upper deck that replaced the awning after the return-from-war service can be seen here.

Isle of Arran at the inner 1A berth, known as the '*Kylemore* berth', at Rothesay, with the funnel of *Eagle III* moored on the outside of the pier behind.

Isle of Arran in the 1920s. (PSPS collection, courtesy Robin Boyd)

Opposite below: Isle of Arran was operated on the Thames on river and docks cruises twice a week and on the other days she sailed to Herne Bay, Margate and the Nore Lightship. In 1933 she sailed with a grey hull, white saloons and paddle boxes and a red black-topped funnel. In 1934 she carried the standard GSNC colours of black hull and buff black-topped funnel. She was withdrawn after the 1936 season and sold for scrapping. She is seen here in September 1934 in the Thames Estuary. (Sidney Perrier, courtesy C.J. Perrier)

Isle of Arran, taken from another steamer, with a Clyde Shipping Co. paddle tug ahead of her. She remained on the Glasgow to Rothesay run, with occasional excursions to Lochgoilhead until replaced by *Queen Mary* in 1933. In May 1933 she was sold to the General Steam Navigation Co. for service on the Thames.

In 1894, when *Eagle* was sold to the Manchester Ship Canal, *Guy Mannering* of the North British Railway was purchased to replace her on the Glasgow to Rothesay service and was renamed *Isle of Bute*. She had been built in 1871 by Caird's as *Sheila* for Gillies & Campbell and purchased by the NB in 1882 and renamed the following year. She had been fitted with an aft deck saloon in 1892 and a fore saloon added around the time she was purchased by Buchanan.

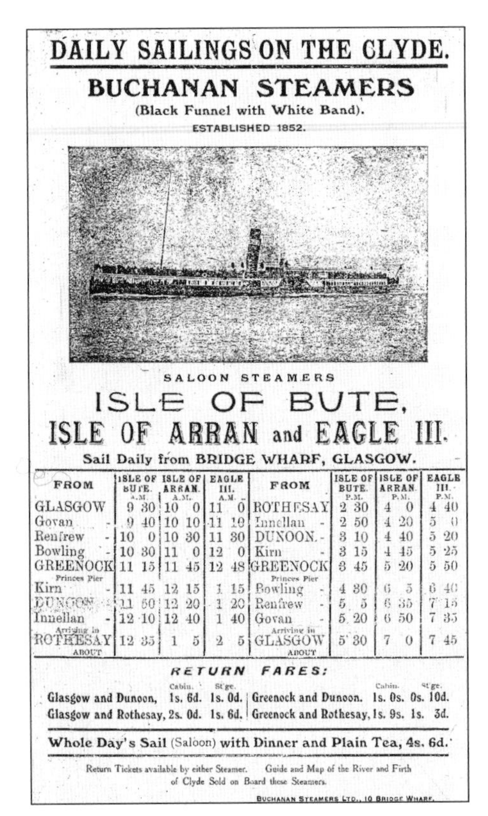

DAILY SAILINGS ON THE CLYDE.

BUCHANAN STEAMERS

(Black Funnel with White Band).

ESTABLISHED 1852.

SALOON STEAMERS

ISLE OF BUTE,

ISLE OF ARRAN and EAGLE III.

Sail Daily from BRIDGE WHARF, GLASGOW.

FROM	ISLE OF BUTE. A.M.	ISLE OF ARRAN. A.M.	EAGLE III. A.M.	FROM	ISLE OF BUTE. P.M.	ISLE OF ARRAN. P.M.	EAGLE III. P.M.
GLASGOW	9 30	10 0	11 0	ROTHESAY	2 30	4 0	4 40
Govan -	9 40	10 10	11 10	Innellan -	2 50	4 20	5 0
Renfrew -	10 0	10 30	11 30	DUNOON -	3 10	4 40	5 20
Bowling -	10 30	11 0	12 0	Kirn -	3 15	4 45	5 25
GREENOCK Princes Pier	11 15	11 45	12 48	GREENOCK Princes Pier	3 45	5 20	5 50
Kirn -	11 45	12 15	1 15	Bowling -	4 30	6 5	6 40
DUNOON -	11 50	12 20	1 20	Renfrew -	5 5	6 35	7 15
Innellan -	12 10	12 40	1 40	Govan -	5 20	6 50	7 35
Arriving in ROTHESAY ABOUT	12 35	1 5	2 5	Arriving in GLASGOW ABOUT	5 30	7 0	7 45

RETURN FARES:

	Cabin.	St'ge.		Cabin.	St'ge.
Glasgow and Dunoon,	1s. 6d.	1s. 0d.	Greenock and Dunoon.	1s. 0s.	0s. 10d.
Glasgow and Rothesay,	2s. 0d.	1s. 6d.	Greenock and Rothesay,	1s. 9s.	1s. 3d.

Whole Day's Sail (Saloon) with Dinner and Plain Tea, 4s. 6d.

Return Tickets available by either Steamer. Guide and Map of the River and Firth of Clyde Sold on Board these Steamers.

BUCHANAN STEAMERS LTD., 10 BRIDGE WHARF.

A handbill from 1910 or 1911, showing the Glasgow to Rothesay sailings by *Isle of Bute*, *Isle of Arran* and *Eagle III*. Note that Bridge Wharf is the renamed Broomielaw, on the north side of the river, and that the Buchanan steamers did not call at Gourock or Craigmore.

Isle of Bute at Govan pier. (CRSC)

Isle of Bute off Anderston Quay. She was sold in July 1912 to Samuel Cordingley of Morecambe. She was damaged by being driven against the pier there shortly after entering service and was sold in October 1913 for breaking up.

In June 1904 *Duchess of York*, the former *Jeanie Deans* of the NB fleet, was purchased and renamed *Isle of Cumbrae*, replacing *Vivid*. (McQueen collection, Glasgow University Archives)

Isle of Cumbrae passing the D. & W. Henderson shipyard at Govan. From 1904 until 1915 she included Saturday afternoon cruises to Garelochhead in her roster. (L.J. Vogt)

Isle of Cumbrae was one of the few Clyde steamers not taken up for war service, and from 1916 to 1919 she was chartered by the Glasgow & South Western Railway, and painted with their funnel colours, as seen here. Although passing into the ownership of Williamson-Buchanan steamers she did not sail for them and was scrapped at Dumbarton in 1920.

In 1910 *Eagle III* joined the fleet. She was ordered from A. & J. Inglis, but the hull was subcontracted to Napier & Miller of Old Kilpatrick, while Inglis constructed her single diagonal machinery and a haystack boiler, the last such to be built for a Clyde steamer. In her first season she was rather unstable, developing a heavy list when large crowds of passengers were on board, and she went back to Inglis for alterations in autumn 1910. These involved increasing her beam below the waterline. (G.E. Langmuir collection, Mitchell Library)

Eagle III normally sailed on the 11:00 run from Glasgow to Rothesay followed by an afternoon cruise to the head of Loch Striven. (CRSC Archive)

A postcard view of *Eagle III* leaving the Broomielaw.

Eagle III arriving at Rothesy in pre-1913 condition with black paddle boxes.

Eagle III leaving Dunoon with white paddle-boxes between 1913 and 1916. After the boom between the Cloch and Dunoon was fitted on 1 July 1915 she continued sailing inside it, from Glasgow to the Holy Loch and to Helensburgh and the Gareloch for the remainder of that summer, and in 1916 from the beginning of the season until she was requisitioned by the Admiralty on 2 June of that year. (CRSC)

In 1917 *Eagle III* was requisitioned for use as a minesweeper. She was based firstly at Grimsby and later at Harwich and is seen here in that guise. (CRSC archive)

In 1920 *Eagle III* emerged after her war service with her bridge moved forward of the funnel, which was now the Williamson-Buchanan white with a black top, and with a small after-deck shelter with seating on the top replacing the earlier awning.

Eagle III in Rothesay Bay in the 1920s. (PSPS collection, courtesy Robin Boyd)

Eagle III continued on the 11:00 sailing to Rothesay until she was replaced by *King Edward* in 1933, on the arrival of *Queen Mary*, when she moved to the 09:30 departure. She is seen here off Ardyne.

NOW.—On Friday, 14th July, SPECIAL SAILINGS at 1.30 p.m. for KIRN, DUNOON, INNELLAN, ROTHESAY, BLAIRMORE, CARRICK CASTLE and LOCHGOILHEAD

FAIR HOLIDAYS

15th till 19th JULY, 1933, inclusive

TO THE COAST

Luxurious White Funnel Steamers sail from Glasgow Bridge Wharf (South Side)

EAGLE (On Monday 17th July only) - at **9** a.m.
For DUNOON and ROTHESAY; due back about 8-0 p.m.

EAGLE (or other steamer) - - at **9.30** a.m.
For DUNOON and ROTHESAY; due back about 8-0 p.m.

NEW TURBINE STEAMER
QUEEN MARY - - at **10** a.m.
For DUNOON, ROTHESAY, LARGS, MILLPORT (Keppel), and CRUISE to ARRAN, etc.; due back 8.30 p.m.

QUEEN-EMPRESS (or Kylemore) - at **10-40** a.m.
For DUNOON, KIRN, BLAIRMORE, CARRICK CASTLE and LOCHGOILHEAD; due back 8.40 p.m.

T.S. **KING EDWARD** - at **11** a.m.
For DUNOON, ROTHESAY, and SPECIAL CRUISE; due back 7.45 p.m.

EAGLE (or Kylemore) - - at B**1.30** p.m.
For DUNOON and ROTHESAY

Returning from Keppel 4.20; Largs 4.40; Rothesay 3.45, 4.40 and 5.30 p.m.; Dunoon 4.25, 5.25, 6.5 and 6.15 p.m. Lochgoilhead 4-45 p.m.

B—*At 1.45 p.m. on Saturday and Except Monday 17th July*

RETURN FARES	1st Cabin	2nd Cabin	Sail (1st Cabin) Dinner with Plain Tea	Sail (1st Cabin) Dinner with High Tea
Dunoon or Blairmore	3/-	2/6	—	—
Rothesay, Largs, Keppel or Lochgoilhead (Day)	3/6	2/6	7/6	8/6
Arran etc. Cruise	5/-	4/-	9/-	10/-
11 a.m. Cruise	4/6	3/6	8/6	9/6

John Williamson & Co., 308 Clyde Street, Glasgow c.1

Above Left: Eagle III offered evening cruises from Glasgow, as in this advertisement from 1931. Note that the numeral was dropped in the advertising, and that John Williamson & Co., not Williamson-Buchanan Steamers, placed the advertisement. (CRSC archive) *Above Right:* A handbill for Williamson-Buchanan's sailings in the Glasgow Fair period in 1933. Note that in 1929 the departure point had been moved across the river from Broomielaw (Bridge Wharf) to Bridge Wharf (South Side) following the opening of King George V Bridge. (CRSC archive)

Eagle III off Dumbuck in Williamson-Buchanan (1936) Ltd colours. In the peak summer months from 1936 to 1939 she sailed on the Glasgow to Lochgoilhead service on three days of the week, prior to that this had been a Sunday duty. (G.E. Langmuir)

Right: A handbill for Williamson-Buchanan sailings for the Glasgow Autumn Holiday in 1936 showing the standard pattern of departures from the mid-to-late thirties. (CRSC archive)

WILLIAMSON - BUCHANAN STEAMERS

AUTUMN HOLIDAY

Monday, 28th September

SAILINGS TO

THE COAST

From GLASGOW BRIDGE WHARF (S.S.)

AS UNDER:

"EAGLE" - - - at 9.0 a.m.

To Dunoon and Rothesay

TURBINE

"QUEEN MARY II" at 10.0 a.m.

To Dunoon, Rothesay, Largs, Millport (Keppel) aud Cruise to Lochranza (Arran)

TURBINE

"KING EDWARD" at 11.0 a.m.

To Kirn, Dunoon, Innellan, Rothesay and Cruise to Kyles of Bute

"KYLEMORE" - at 1.30 p.m.

To Kirn, Dunoon, Innellan and Rothesay

Steamers return from Keppel 4.10 p.m., Largs 4.30 p.m., Rothesay 4.40 and 5.30 p.m., Dunoon 5.25 and 6.5 p.m.

RETURN FARES	Saloon	3rd Class	Saloon with Lunch & High Tea	Saloon with Lunch & Plain Tea
DUNOON - - - - - -	3/-	2/-	—	—
ROTHESAY, LARGS or KEPPEL -	3/6	2/6	8/6	7/6
LOCHRANZA CRUISE - - -	5/-	4/-	10/-	9/-
DAY'S SAIL per 11 a.m. Steamer -	4/6	3/6	9/6	8/6

SUNDAY SAILINGS

11 a.m. per T.S. "Queen Mary II"; 2.15 p.m. per T.S. "King Edward"

For T.S. "Queen Mary II" Saturday Sailing see over

Passengers are referred to the Sailing Conditions on board the Steamers.

McCorquodale & Co. Ltd., Glasgow, London, etc.

Opposite below: The purchase of Williamson-Buchanan steamers by the LMSR in October 1935 saw little change in *Eagle III*'s appearance, with the brown paint on the ventilators being replaced by silver paint. She is seen here arriving at Dunoon.

Eagle III at Rothesay between 1937 and 1939 with the 1937 *Juno* behind her.

Eagle III took evacuees from Gartnavel mental hospital from Glasgow to Ardrishaig on 28 August 1939. She was requisitioned for minesweeping in October of that year and served as *HMS Oriole*. She was present at Dunkirk and was run up on the beach there at low tide, where she is seen here, to help board the long lines of soldiers. She made five trips there and, remarkably, survived. (G.E. Langmuir collection, Mitchell Library)

Eagle III was later used as an accommodation ship and is seen here laid up in the Holy Loch in April 1946. (A. Ernest Glen collection)

Eagle III, with her antiquated single-cylinder engine and haystack boiler, was not refurbished. Had she had a more modern boiler, it is possible that a new boiler would have been ordered for her and she would have returned to service, but none of the Clyde yards was able to construct a haystack boiler at that time. She was sold in August 1946 to Smith & Houston of Port Glasgow for scrapping, seen here with the IOMSP's *Snaefell* (originally Laird Line's *Viper* from the Ardrossan to Belfast service) behind her. (A. Ernest Glen collection)

In March 1913, Buchanan purchased the former Caledonian Steam Packet steamer *Madge Wildfire*, naming her *Isle of Skye*. Cameron of Dumbarton had operated her for the previous two seasons. *Isle of Skye* continued to sail during the summer of 1915, making a daily cruise from Glasgow to Garelochhead. (A. Ernest Glen collection)

Isle of Skye at Port Bannatyne Pier in 1919, with a Williamson-Buchanan funnel.

A side-on view of *Isle of Skye* in Williamson-Buchanan colours. (From a CRSC calendar, G.E. Langmuir collection)

Isle of Skye approaching Rothesay in the same colours. In 1927 she was sold to the Grangemouth & Forth Towing Co. for excursion service on the Forth as *Fair Maid*. She came back to the Clyde during the Second World War as a tender and decontamination vessel and was broken up at Troon in December 1945.

Two
Williamson Steamers

Following the end of the partnership with William Buchanan, Alexander Williamson purchased *Sultan* on 28 February 1862. Barclay Curle had built *Sultan* the previous year for the Glasgow to Kilmun service of Alex McKellar and she had been fitted with the engines of *Wellington* of 1853, constructed by J. Barr. She ran from the Kyles of Bute and Rothesay to the Broomielaw for Alexander Williamson, an upriver service that later became the preserve of *Kylemore*. The remainder of her story, and those of the other three of Alexander Williamson's steamers, are told in *Glasgow and South Western and Other Steamers* and *MacBrayne Steamers*. She is seen here racing *Chancellor*.

Robertson & Co. of Greenock built *Sultana* for Alexander Williamson in 1868 with single diagonal machinery by William King & Co. She also served on the Rothesay service and, from 1869, called at Greenock Princes Pier, providing railway connections with the GSWR. In the 1870s she operated a direct service from Princes Pier to Rothesay, with, on certain days, an afternoon excursion round Bute.

Viceroy was the third steamer to join what was by now known as the 'Turkish Fleet'. Not only did the steamers have Turkish names but the house flag echoed the Turkish flag with a yellow star and crescent on a blue ground. She was built in 1875 by D. &W. Henderson at Partick and is seen here in GSWR colours. She had single diagonal machinery by Hutson & Corbett, which was converted to a two-cylinder arrangement in 1886. (Douglas McGowan collection)

In 1889 *Marquis of Bute* was purchased on behalf of the creditors of Captain McLean. She is seen here at the Broomielaw with *Petrel* inboard of her, the bow of *Dunoon Castle* in the right foreground, and *Loch Lomond* to the right of *Marquis of Bute*'s funnel. This picture must have been taken in 1868, as *Loch Lomond* was laid up after that season. *Marquis of Bute* had been built in that year by Barclay Curle and later ran on the Greenock Princes Pier to Rothesay service.

Marquis of Bute after a short aft-saloon was added in 1891. By the 1880s three of Alexander Williamson's sons – Alexander (Jr), James, and John – were captains on his steamers. All three went on to make a major mark in Clyde steamer history. James became a partner in the Frith of Clyde Steam Packet Co., owners of the teetotal steamer *Ivanhoe*, in 1880, and Marine Superintendent of the Caledonian Steam Packet Co. on 1888. In 1891 Alexander Williamson (Sr) sold his 'Turkish Fleet' to the GSWR and Alexander (Jr) went with the steamers to become that company's Marine Superintendent.

After Alexander Williamson retired in 1891, his son John set up in business on his own account as a steamer owner. His first purchase was *Benmore* (see Chapter One) in the autumn of the same year from William Buchanan. She was moved to a Rothesay-based service rather than a Glasgow-based one, with extensions to the Kyles of Bute on two or three days per week in the winter months. Note the two vehicles, probably coaches (although the aft one may be a horseless carriage) forward of the funnel in this illustration, which dates from 1896, when the paddle boxes and boats were painted white, to 1898, when the funnel became white with a black top. (CRSC)

Benmore with the white black-topped funnel carried after 1898, passing Connell's shipyard. In summer 1903 she operated a service from Helensburgh, Kilcreggan, Strone and Kirn to Dunoon, starting on certain days from Garelochhead, connecting with the Turbine Steamers at Dunoon. Special trips saw her sail on occasion to Inveraray, Lochranza, Carradale, and Campbeltown, the latter three to relieve *King Edward* in the peak season of 1901. (CRSC

Benmore continued sailing from Glasgow until summer 1915, when she was on a service from Kirn and Dunoon to Glasgow. From 1916 to 1920 she was chartered to the Caledonian Steam Packet because almost all the latter company's steamers had been called up for war duty. She ran from Wemyss Bay to Millport and also, on occasion, on the Holy Loch service. She is seen here in mid-firth on Glasgow Autumn Holiday, 27 September 1919. (CRSC archive)

On 30 September 1920, *Benmore* returned to service for Williamson-Buchanan, as the company had now become, and the Glasgow to Rothesay service. On 19 October she was laid up because of the threat of a miner's strike, then was damaged by fire on 11 November in Greenock's East India Harbour and never sailed again. On 4 May 1923 Captain John Williamson died and in October of that year *Benmore* was sold for breaking up at Dumbarton. She is seen here after the fire in the East India Harbour, alongside MacBrayne's *Grenadier*. (CRSC Archive)

In 1892 John Williamson purchased *Sultan* from the GSWR. She was renamed *Ardmore* by him, and is seen here off Greenock, but she did not remain under his ownership for long and was sold after about a year to David MacBrayne and became their *Gairlochy* on the Loch Ness service.

In 1895, *Glenmore* was built for John Williamson by Messrs Russell of Port Glasgow with compound diagonal machinery by Rankin & Blackmore. She is seen here in her first season in tRothesy Bay. (Douglas Brown collection)

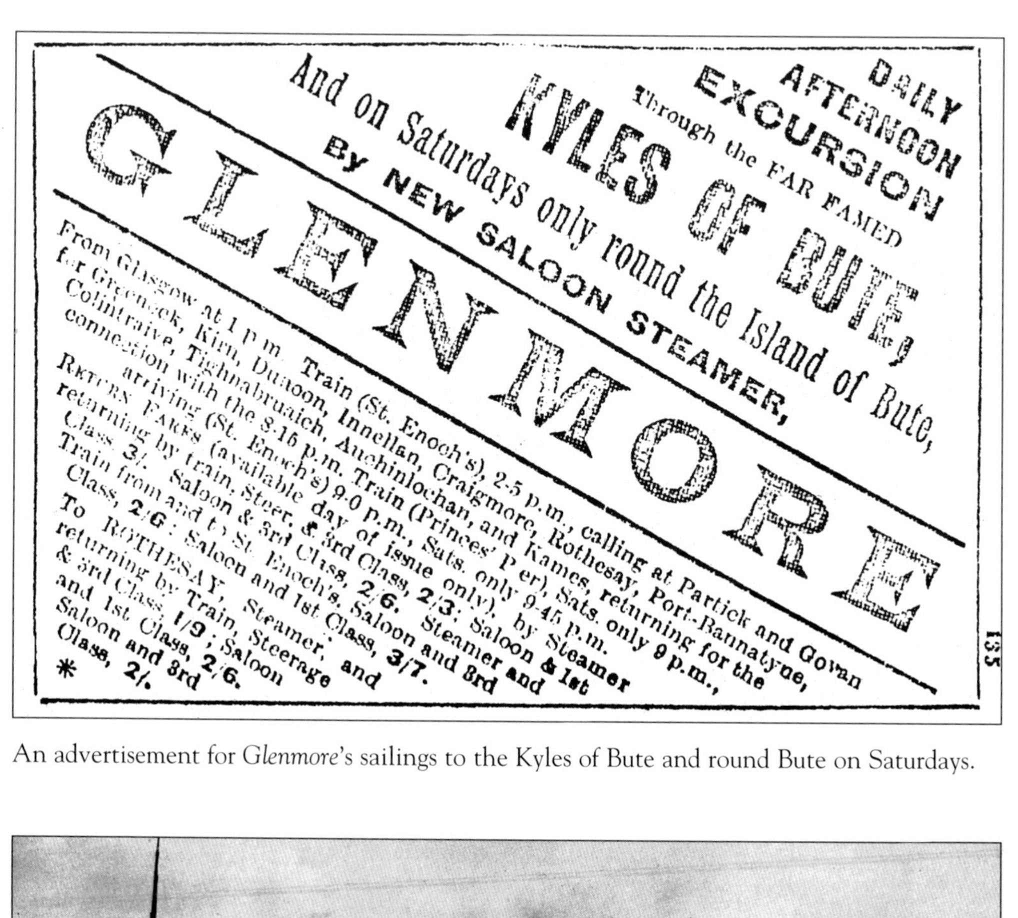

An advertisement for *Glenmore*'s sailings to the Kyles of Bute and round Bute on Saturdays.

Glenmore, seen here off the mouth of Holy Loch, was sold during her second summer to a Captain Wiggins for an expedition to the River Yenesei in Siberia. She sailed there along with the Tay steamer *Scotia* in August 1896. She wintered at the Norwegian port of Vardö after arriving there on 25 August and finding that the other ships in the party had gone on ahead, along with their escorting icebreaker. In August 1897 she sailed on to Siberia, reaching the mouth of the Yenesei on the 23rd of that month. She was purchased there by a local firm and renamed *Oryol* or *Orel*, but her ultimate fate is unknown, although she was reported still to be sailing in 1943. (CRSC collection)

In 1896, Williamson purchased *Sultana* from the GSWR. She was sold again in 1899 to the Lochfyne & Glasgow Steam Packet Co. Ltd.

A view of the river at the Broomielaw between 1896 and 1899, with *Sultana*, in Williamson colours, in mid-river and *Benmore* and *Iona* at the quay. *Clutha No.7* is heading upstream and *Clutha No.1* is heading downstream, off *Sultana*. (Annan Photographers)

Strathmore replaced the departed *Glenmore* in 1897. Russell & Co. built her, like her predecessor, with compound machinery by Rankin & Blackmore. She differed in being plated up to the bow. (Douglas Brown collection)

Strathmore in white funnel condition post-1898. She mainly served on the Glasgow to Rothesay and the Kyles service, although from 1898 to 1900, as a precursor of *King Edward*, she maintained a service from Fairlie to Campbeltown. (Robin Boyd collection)

Strathmore approaching Largs. (CRSC)

In March 1908, *Strathmore* was replaced by *Kylemore* and was sold to the Admiralty and renamed *Harlequin* for service as a tender-cum-ferry on the Medway at the naval bases at Chatham and Sheerness. She served as a minesweeper, based at Swansea, in the First World War. Her end came when she was stranded in 1943 in the Medway. She was broken up in 1945.

A sister ship to *Strathmore*, to be named *Kylemore*, was ordered from Russell & Co. in 1897, but was sold whilst on the stocks to the Hastings, St Leonards-on-Sea and Eastbourne Steamboat Co. She sailed for them as *Britannia* and was sold back to John Williamson in 1904. He immediately sold her to the GSWR and she became their *Vulcan*. In April 1908, John Williamson took ownership of her for the third time, and she regained the name she was originally intended to have, *Kylemore*. She is seen here off Greenock. (Douglas McGowan collection)

Kylemore passing *HMS Cumberland*. In 1915 she was taken up by the Admiralty as a minesweeper, being based first at Dunkirk and then at Harwich.

On reconditioning after her return from war in 1919, *Kylemore* had her bridge moved forward of her funnel. She is seen here at Dunoon from *Columba*. (CRSC)

A smoky, filled to capacity *Kylemore*, sailing down river. Her afternoon trip from Glasgow made a popular afternoon excursion, returning from Dunoon by *Isle of Arran* (or *King Edward* after 1927).

Kylemore off Greenock Princes Pier. Her main service, throughout her life, was on the Rothesay to Glasgow service, departing Rothesay in the morning and returning at 14:00. (F.A. Plant)

Kylemore leaving Glasgow in the 1920s. (From a CRSC calendar, Stromier Vogt collection)

Kylemore offered a variety of evening cruises during the summer months, as in this handbill from Rothesay and Craigmore for August 1932.

POPULAR

Evening Cruises

(WEATHER FAVOURABLE)

BY MAGNIFICENT STEAMER

"KYLEMORE"

	FROM ROTHESAY	FROM CRAIGM'RE
Saturdays, 13th and 20th August. **LARGS and DUNOON** (About 2½ hours at LARGS or 1 hour at DUNOON)	6-30	6-35
DUNOON direct by "King Edward" (Time on shore and back per "KYLEMORE")	6-15	—
Monday, 15th August. **DUNOON & CARRICK CASTLE** (Time on shore at DUNOON or CARRICK CASTLE)	6-45	—
Tuesday, 16th August. **Largs, Millport & Corrie (Arran)** (Passengers may land at Largs or Millport and rejoin Steamer on return journey)	7-0	7-5
Wednesday, 17th August. **Largs, Millport and Kilchattan Bay** (Passengers may land at LARGS, MILLPORT or KILCHATTAN BAY)	7-0	7-5
Thursday, 18th August. **LARGS, MILLPORT & BRODICK** (Passengers may land at LARGS or MILLPORT and rejoin Steamer on return journey.)	6-0	—
Friday, 19th August. **MYSTERY CRUISE** (Dancing on Board and on Shore) PORT-BANNATYNE 7-15	7-0	7-5

MUSIC ON BOARD

CRUISE FARE - - - - - 1/9
Largs, Millport or Dunoon (direct) - - 1/6
Dunoon (via Largs) - - - - - - 1/9

JOHN WILLIAMSON & CO., 308 Clyde Street, Glasgow, C.1.

John Horn, Ltd., Glasgow and London.

POPULAR

EVENING CRUISES

(WEATHER FAVOURABLE)

BY STEAMER

"KYLEMORE"

	FROM LARGS	FROM MILLPORT (OLD PIER)
Saturday 1st July **DUNOON** (Allowing about 1 Hour on Shore)	7-15	—
Monday 3rd July **ROUND DRU'KEN ISLAND**	7-25	7-45

MUSIC ON BOARD

CRUISE FARES:

DUNOON - - - - - 1/6
DRU'KEN ISLAND - - 1/9

JOHN WILLIAMSON & Co., 308 Clyde Street, Glasgow, C.1.

John Horn, Ltd., Glasgow and London.

A handbill for evening cruises from Largs and Millport by *Kylemore* for July 1933. Dru'ken (Drunken) Island is Inchmarnock.

POPULAR

EVENING CRUISES

(WEATHER FAVOURABLE)

BY STEAMER

"KYLEMORE"

From DUNOON 7-30

MONDAY, 14th AUGUST,

Carrick Castle

(TIME ON SHORE)

WEDNESDAY, 16th AUGUST,

HELENSBURGH

(TIME ON SHORE)

MUSIC ON BOARD

Cruise Fare - 1/6

JOHN WILLIAMSON & Co., 306 Clyde Street, Glasgow, C.1

John Horn, Ltd., Glasgow and London.

A handbill for evening cruises from Dunoon by *Kylemore*, including one to Carrick Castle to land for August 1933.

Kylemore in Rothesay Bay. In addition to her scheduled service she also operated as a tender to Atlantic liners moored at the tail of the bank. The takeover by the LMSR made little difference to her sailings.

Kylemore at the inside 1A berth at Rothesay between 1920 and 1924, a berth which was her home and which is known to this day as 'the *Kylemore* berth'. (PSPS collection, courtesy Robin Boyd)

Kylemore off Dunoon. In December 1939 she was again requisitioned as a minesweeper, and also used as a netlayer. She was sunk by bombing off Harwich whilst minesweeping on 21 August 1936.

In 1900 John Williamson purchased the small coaster *Alert*, and placed her on a cargo and luggage service to Rothesay. She had been built by J. Fullerton & Co. at Paisley in 1898 as a fish-carrying steamer for Smith & Ritchie. She only lasted a short while in the Williamson fleet. After she was sold, the puffer *Stormlight* was chartered for a while, but the advent of *King Edward* meant that *Strathmore* could be moved back to the Glasgow-based sailings.

Alert was sold to German owners in May or June 1901 and renamed *Skirner*, and was rebuilt to a cargo-passenger steamer. She was registered at Sonderburg, which was then German, but is now Sønderborg in Denmark. In 1925 she was converted to a motorship. She was in Danish ownership by this time and was renamed to *Sakskjøbing* in 1928 and again to *Pollux* in 1933. On 28 November 1940 she was lost between Hasle and Bandholm, probably through striking a mine.

Queen-Empress, seen here off Gourock, was the final paddle steamer to join the fleet of John Williamson. She was built by Murdoch & Murray at Port Glasgow in 1912, and was an updated version of the CSP's *Duchess of Fife*, but with the main deck plated to the bow. She had compound diagonal engines, again by Rankin & Blackmore, and similar, although larger then, to those on *Maid of the Loch*. She presented quite a contrast with the anachronistic *Eagle III*, built for Buchanan only two years previously.

Queen-Empress was the last Clyde Steamer to be built before the fateful year of 1914. She effectively replaced *Benmore* in Williamson's fleet, relegating the latter to cargo runs and special and relief passenger sailings. In 1913 she made a special sailing from Ayr to Arrochar and in 1914 was on the morning Rothesay to Glasgow run that later became the preserve of *Kylemore*. She is seen here off Toward.

Queen-Empress served in the First World War as a troop transport out of Southampton and later as a minesweeper. She remained in Admiralty service after the war, as a hospital ship in the Archangel campaign in support of the White Russians. Whilst there she ran aground and was pulled off in the nick of time as the Bolsheviks approached. She did not resume Clyde service until 1920, and is seen here refitting for that service, with the burnt-out *Benmore* aft of her and *Queen Alexandra* in dry dock to her right.

Queen-Empress, seen here off Gourock Pier, returned to Clyde sailings in 1920 with all-day trips during the Glasgow Fair from Glasgow to Ayr or Campbeltown. This latter sailing was so long that only fifteen minutes were allowed ashore at the Kintyre capital. In 1920, and from 1922 to 1935, she took the Campbeltown sailings normally taken by *King Edward* and by *Queen Alexandra* after 1927 (in September when the turbine had been laid up for the winter). The year 1928 was an exception to this as she was on charter to David MacBrayne for the Ardrishaig mail service and *Eagle III* took the Campbeltown sailings

Queen-Empress offered downriver sailings, sometimes relieving *Eagle III* on the 11:00 sailing to Rothesay, but also to Lochgoilhead in the 1920s and early 1930s. She is seen here after 1929 leaving Bridge Wharf (South Side) with *King Edward* moored further down.

Queen-Empress also offered long day excursions on selected dates from Helensburgh and Dunoon, as in this handbill from August 1931. The sailing to Campbeltown via the Kyles is not one that has been repeated in more recent years amongst the wide variety of cruises operated by *Waverley*, or special charters by the Clyde River Steamer Club and other enthusiast organisations. This cruise returned via Pladda and Largs, with passengers for the Kyles piers changing at *Kylemore* at Rothesay, which called at Tighnabruaich in the course of an evening cruise.

SPECIAL EXCURSIONS

(Weather favourable)

BY MAGNIFICENT STEAMER

QUEEN-EMPRESS

On MONDAY, 24th AUGUST.

To Brodick, Lamlash, Whiting Bay (ARRAN)

and thence to

CAMPBELTOWN

(Allowing 1 hour on Shore)

from

HELENSBURGH	8-30 a.m.	LARGS	9-40 a.m.
DUNOON	9-5 ,,	MILLPORT (Old Pier)	10-0 ,,

Passengers may land at Arran Ports and rejoin Steamer on return.
Due back Millport about 6-50, Largs 7-10, Dunoon 7-45, Helensburgh 8-15 p.m.

On TUESDAY, 25th AUGUST.

To INVERARAY (Allowing time on Shore)

from

HELENSBURGH	8-30 a.m.	LARGS	9-55 a.m.
DUNOON	9-5 ,,	MILLPORT (Old Pier)	10-25 ,,

Due back Millport about 5-30, Largs 6-0, Dunoon 6-45, Helensburgh 7-30 p.m.

On WEDNESDAY, 26th AUGUST.

To AYR (Allowing about 2 hours Ashore)

from

HELENSBURGH	8-40 a.m.	CRAIGMORE	10-10 a.m.
KIRN	9-15 ,,	ROTHESAY	10-15 ,,
DUNOON	9-30 ,,	LARGS	10-50 ,,
INNELLAN	9-50 ,,	MILLPORT (Old Pier)	11-15 ,,

Due back Millport about 5-0, Largs 5-20, Rothesay 6-0, Dunoon 6-40, Helensburgh 7-30 p.m.

On THURSDAY, 27th AUGUST.

To CAMPBELTOWN

(Landing for about 1 Hour).

Via Far-Famed KYLES OF BUTE and Round the Islands of BUTE, ARRAN and CUMBRAE

from

HELENSBURGH	8-30 a.m.	ROTHESAY	10-20 a.m.
DUNOON	9-5 ,,	COLINTRAIVE	11-0 ,,
LARGS	9-40 ,,	TIGHNABRUAICH	11-15 ,,
CRAIGMORE	10-15 ,,	KAMES	11-25 ,,

Allowing Passengers about 1 hour at Campbeltown, and due back Largs 6-0, Rothesay 6-45, Dunoon 7-30, Helensburgh 8-0 p.m.

Kyles Passengers return from Rothesay per "Kylemore" at 7-0 p.m.

On FRIDAY, 28th AUGUST.

TO ARRAN

from

HELENSBURGH	8-30 a.m.	ROTHESAY	10-0 a.m.
DUNOON	9-5 ,,	LARGS	10-30 ,,
CRAIGMORE	9-45 ,,	MILLPORT (Old Pier)	10-50 ,,

Direct to BRODICK, LAMLASH and WHITING BAY.

Passengers may have about 3 hours ashore at Brodick, 2 at Lamlash, or 1¼ at Whiting Bay.

Steamer due back Millport (Old Pier) 4-20, Largs 4-40, Craigmore 5-15, Rothesay 5-20, Dunoon 6-0, Helensburgh 6-45 p.m.

SPECIAL EXCURSION

(WEATHER FAVOURABLE)

BY MAGNIFICENT STEAMER

"Queen-Empress"

WEDNESDAY, 26th JULY

To GIRVAN

and CRUISE

Round Ailsa Craig

Passengers may have about 2 hours Ashore at GIRVAN and rejoin Steamer at 4-0 p.m.

	Depart	Due back
Brodick	11-40 a.m.	6-15 p.m.
Lamlash	12-10 p.m.	5-50 p.m.
Whiting Bay	12-30 p.m.	5-30 p.m.

Cheap Return Fares:

Saloon, 3/-; Fore-Saloon, 2/-

JOHN WILLIAMSON & Co., 308 Clyde Street, Glasgow, C.1.

JOHN HORN, LTD., GLASGOW.

A handbill from July 1933 for a sailing by *Queen-Empress* from the east Arran piers to Girvan and round Ailsa Craig.

SPECIAL EXCURSION

(Weather Favourable)

WEDNESDAY, 11th JULY

By Luxurious Steamer

"Queen-Empress"

ROUND

AILSA CRAIG

From

Girvan at 1.15 p.m.

Due back at 3.15 p.m.

Return Fare - - - 1/6

John Williamson & Co., 308 Clyde Street, Glasgow, C.1.

Sam Lithgow, Printer, Glasgow.

The section of that sailing from Girvan round Ailsa Craig was offered as an afternoon cruise, as in this handbill from July 1934.

Special Afternoon

SUNDAY EXCURSION

—: to view :—

No. 534

The New Cunarder being built at Clydebank

Sunday First, 12th Aug.

By Saloon Steamer

"Queen-Empress"

From	Depart	Due Back
ROTHESAY, - -	1.15	5.50
INNELLAN, - - -	1.30	5.25
DUNOON, - - -	1.55	5.5
KIRN, - - - -	2.0	5.0

Afternoon Return Fare, - 2/6

John Williamson & Co., 308 Clyde Street, Glasgow, C.1

Sam Lithgow, Printer, Glasgow.

August 1934 also saw an upriver sailing to see the Cunarder 534 (*Queen Mary*) under construction at John Brown's yard at Clydebank from Rothesay, Innellan, Dunoon and Kirn.

Queen-Empress departing from Kirn. (CRSC)

A stern view of a lightly-loaded *Queen-Empress* in the 1920s. (PSPS collection, courtesy Robin Boyd)

QUEEN EMPRESS

Above: After the takeover by the LMSR in October 1935, *Queen-Empress* was moved to the Wemyss Bay to Rothesay service. She is seen here from *Queen Mary II* at Rothesay after 1937, with *Juno* approaching. (CRSC)

Right: A handbill for evening cruises from Fairlie, Millport (both Keppel and Old Piers) and Kilchattan Bay for August 1938.

Opposite: *Queen-Empress* at Girvan in 1923. Around the hull is a blue mourning band for John Williamson, who had died earlier that year. (CRSC)

PLEASE RETAIN THIS HANDBILL FOR REFERENCE

B 16581

WILLIAMSON-BUCHANAN STEAMERS

Evening Cruises

By P.S. "QUEEN-EMPRESS"

Tuesday, 16th August

To DUNOON

Allowing about 1 Hour on Shore

Thursday, 18th August

To BRODICK (Arran)

Allowing time on shore

	p.m.
From FAIRLIE	6 30
,, MILLPORT (Keppel Pier)	6 38
,, ,, (Old Pier)	6 45
,, KILCHATTAN BAY	7 10

Arriving back at Fairlie 9.50, Keppel 10.0, Millport 10.10 and Kilchattan Bay 10.30 p.m.

RETURN FARES

DUNOON	1/8
BRODICK	1/11

CHILDREN HALF-FARE

Passengers are referred to the Sailing Conditions published on board the Steamers.

August, 1938
E.R.O. 53302
ZD—11/8/38—No. 1—650—McCorquodale, Glasgow.

In March 1938 *Queen-Empress* had her funnel painted in the CSP colours of yellow, with a black top. From 1939 she was on the Wemyss Bay and Fairlie to Millport and Rothesay runs along with *Duchess of Fife*. She is seen here leaving Dunoon.

Queen-Empress approaching Millport on 17 August 1939, with her yellow funnel clearly visible. From 7 to 21 September 1939, after the boom was placed in position from Dunoon to the Cloch, she had a spell on the Holy Loch service. On 28 October 1939 she was again taken over by the Admiralty, and became flagship of the 12th Minesweeping Flotilla, based at Portsmouth. She is credited with bringing down two enemy aircraft. She was not re-conditioned after the war and was sold for scrapping in Holland in August 1946. (Douglas Brown collection)

three

The Lochgoil Steamers

INVERARY, LOCHLOMOND, &c.

On WEDNESDAY the 2d of JUNE,

THE ST. GEORGE & ST. CATHERINE Steam-Boats will commence to ply daily betwixt GLASGOW & LOCHGOILHEAD, & ARROCHAR, when, by them,—a COACH running between LOCHGOILHEAD & St. CATHERINE'S—and a STEAM BOAT on the Ferry between ST. CATHERINE'S and INVERARY—Passengers will be conveyed as follow:—

TO INVERARY FROM GLASGOW

Every Morning, as follows:—On Tuesdays, Wednesdays, Thursdays, and Fridays, at Seven o'Clock; on *Saturdays* at Six o'Clock, and on *Mondays* at an hour to be seen on the boards.

FROM INVERARY TO GLASGOW

Every Forenoon, at an hour to suit the tide in the Clyde, so as to make the passage as expeditious as possible, which will be seen on the board at Inverary.

By this route the journey betwixt Glasgow and Inverary is generally accomplished within seven hours.

TO LOCHLOMOND FROM GLASGOW,

BY THE STEAM-BOAT TO ARROCHAR,

Every Morning, at an hour to be seen on the boards.

FROM LOCHLOMOND AND ARROCHAR

Every Afternoon.

Either the ST. GEORGE or ST. CATHERINE will leave GLASGOW for GOUROCK, ARDENTENNIE, and LOCHGOILHEAD *Every Saturday Afternoon,* and return early on Monday morning.

Not having been supported by the public in their attempt to keep the fares at a rate sufficient to preserve a proper distinction and separation between the Cabin and Steerage Passengers, *the Owners of these Boats have been obliged to reduce their fares to the same rate as in other Boats.*

The Lochgoil & Lochlong Steamboat Co. was founded in 1825. They took over *Oscar*, which had been on the route since 1818 and had been built at Dundee in 1814 as *Tay* for service on that river. She was wrecked off Roseneath Point in 1831. *St Catherine* was built in 1825 by John Wood at Port Glasgow, and *St George* in 1826 by J.H. Ritchie and John Wood at Port Glasgow. The Lochgoil route was part of the main route from Glasgow to Inveraray for many years with passengers travelling to Lochgoilhead by steamer, on to St Catherine's by horse-drawn coach and thence to Inveraray by ferry across Loch Fyne. *St George* was also advertised about this time for a cruise to the Kyles of Bute and, 'should the weather permit, round the island of Bute'. It will be seen from the adjacent advertisement that the Lochgoil steamers also served Arrochar. (G.E. Langmuir collection, Mitchell Library)

INVERARAY,
ARROCHAR,
LOCHLOMOND, &c.

THE  LOCHGOIL

CONTINUES to Ply Daily to and from LOCHGOIL-HEAD, conveying Passengers between GLASGOW and INVERARAY as usual.

THE ST. CATHERINE

Will Sail from GLASGOW for ARROCHAR every SATURDAY till further notice, at half-past 3 o'clock afternoon, and on TUESDAYS and THURSDAYS at three quarters past 7 o'clock morning, and on WEDNESDAYS and FRIDAYS at half-past 7 o'clock; leaving Arrochar on Monday morning at 6 o'clock, and on Tuesdays, Wednesdays, Thursdays and Fridays, at 4 o'clock afternoon, so as to admit of Passengers returning to Glasgow by Lochlong, after having Sailed up Lochlomond in the morning.

25th June, 1835. GRAHAM, PRINTER

St George ceased operating in about 1829, but *St Catherine* was still in service in 1835, probably her last season of operation. 1835 was the first season of the first *Loch Goil*, built by Tod & McGregor at Mavisbank with machinery by Robert Napier. At this time *St Catherine* served Arrochar and *Lochgoil*, Lochgoilhead. (G.E. Langmuir collection, Mitchell Library)

The second *Loch Goil* was built in 1841 at an unknown yard, the previous steamer of the same name having presumably been lost or broken up. Details here are sketchy and it is possible that she may have been a rebuild of the 1835 *Loch Goil*.

An early engraving of Lochgoilhead showing *St George* or *St Catherine* arriving at the rudimentary jetty that was used prior to the building of the pier in 1850. (G.E. Langmuir collection, Mitchell Library)

The first *Loch Long* was the first Iron Steamer to be built for Firth of Clyde services. She was built by William Craig & Co. in 1842. In 1847 she was chartered to the Furness Railway Co. for the Barrow to Liverpool service, being renamed *Helveyllyn*, and was purchased by them in the following year. She remained in service until 1867. (G.E. Langmuir collection, Mitchell Library)

Breadalbane replaced *Loch Long* in 1847, being built by Smith & Rodger at Govan. She was sold to Australian owners in November 1856. There she operated from Melbourne to Williamstown, and also as a tug/tender. She later moved to Brisbane and, in 1862, to Sydney where she served on the Manly ferry, and as a cargo ferry after 1871, until she was broken up in 1882. (G.E. Langmuir collection, Mitchell Library)

INVERARY VIA LOCHGOILHEAD.

STEAM CONVEYANCE

TO

AND FROM

Glasgow, Greenock, Gourock, Kilcreggan, Cove,
Ardentinny, & Lochgoilhead;

WITH PASSENGERS TO AND FROM INVERARY.

THE FINE STEAMER,

"**BREADALBANE,**"................ CAPTAIN GRAHAM,
SAILS FROM GLASGOW BRIDGE
Every Morning at Half-past 8 o'clock.---Train at 9.
FOR GREENOCK, GOUROCK, KILCREGGAN, COVE,
ARDENTINNY AND LOCHGOILHEAD;
Arriving at the latter place about HALF-PAST TWELVE o'clock.

At LOCHGOILHEAD, a First-Class and

COMMODIOUS NEW COACH

Waits the arrival of the "*BREADALBANE*," conveying Passengers to ST. CATHERINE'S, a distance of Seven Miles (passing through Scenery unsurpassed for its wild and romantic grandeur), where there is a regular Steamboat Communication across Lochfine to INVERARY.
Passengers for GLASGOW, &c., leave INVERARY, per Steamer "*ARGYLE*," every Forenoon at 10 o'clock, arriving in GLASGOW about Half-past 5 p.m.

The whole distance is accomplished between Glasgow and Inverary in Six Hours.
Passengers from INVERARY, &c., for EDINBURGH, can arrive there at Half-past 7 p.m.

Between INVERARY and OBAN there is a Daily Coach Communication, leaving both places at 9 Morning.

PLEASURE PARTIES

Going and Returning same day from Glasgow, Greenock, or Gourock, to Kilcreggan, Cove, Ardentinny, or Lochgoilhead, charged only One Fare.

FARES:

From GLASGOW to LOCHGOILHEAD, ...Cabin, 2s. 0d.; Steerage, 1s. 6d.
" GREENOCK or GOUROCK to Do.,, " 1s. 6d.; " 1s. 0d.
GLASGOW, June, 1851.

An advertisement for sailings by *Breadalbane* in 1851, featuring a 'commodious new coach', connecting from Lochgoilhead to St Catherine's. (G.E. Langmuir collection, Mitchell Library)

Ardentinny was built in 1851 by T. Wingate & Co. at Whiteinch and was sold in 1858 to owners at Londonderry. She lasted there until 1864 and was renamed *Golden Pledge* for blockade-running, although there is no evidence that she actually crossed the Atlantic. (G.E. Langmuir collection, Mitchell Library)

Steam and Coach
Conveyance
between

GLASGOW AND INVERARY,

Via LOCHGOILHEAD.

THE FINE STEAMER,

LOCHGOIL, - - - - Captain M'Intyre,

SAILS FROM GLASGOW BRIDGE

Every Lawful Morning at Half-past Eight o'clock,

TRAIN TO GREENOCK AT NINE,

FOR LOCHGOILHEAD,

(*With Passengers for Inverary*), *calling at Greenock, Gourock, Kilcreggan, Cove, Portenstuck, and Ardentinny going and returning.*

At LOCHGOILHEAD a splendid and efficiently appointed *Four-Horse Coach* awaits the arrival of the Steamer, by which passengers are conveyed to *ST. CATHERINES*, on the Banks of *LOCHFINE*—a distance of *Seven Miles*—thence by the Co.'s Steamer ARGYLE, across the Loch to Inverary.

The ARGYLE leaves Inverary every Morning at 10 o'clock, with Passengers for *GLASGOW* and other points on the route.

The whole distance between Glasgow and Inverary, and *vice versa*, is accomplished in about six hours.

Pleasure Parties

By the Lochgoil from Glasgow, *or any of the Intermediate Places*, to LOCHGOILHEAD, going and returning same day, charged only ONE FARE, viz.:—

FARES —From GLASGOW to LOCHGOILHEAD, Cabin, 2s; Steerage, 1s. 6d.
From GREENOCK or GOUROCK to LOCHGOILHEAD, Cabin, 1s. 6d.; Steerage, 1s.

An advertisement for sailings by the third *Loch Goil*. (G.E. Langmuir collection, Mitchell Library)

The third *Loch Goil*, built in 1853 by J. Barr, was the first iron steamer on the route, all the previous ones having been wooden-hulled. In 1872 she was sold to the Clyde tug-owners Steele & Bennie for their newly-opened Londonderry operation. She served there until 1877 as *Lough Foyle* and then returned to the Clyde, operating to the Gareloch and later for Henry Sharp as a 'Sunday Breaker'. (G.E. Langmuir collection, Mitchell Library)

In 1882 *Lough Foyle* was purchased by David MacBrayne and became his first *Loch Ness*, serving on the *Loch Ness* mail run from Inverness to Fort Augustus until broken up in 1912. She is seen here at Inverness. By this time she had acquired deck saloons.

A second *Loch Long* followed in 1859 from Alexander Denny of Dumbarton, She was a more modern-looking steamer with a straight stem and the funnel forward of the paddles. In 1864 she was reportedly sold to Copenhagen owners. (G.E. Langmuir collection, Mitchell Library)

Carrick Castle came from Fullerton of Paisley, with single diagonal machinery by W. King & Co., in 1870. She is seen here leaving the Broomielaw passing *Benmore*. She was the first Clyde steamer to have her bridge forward of the funnel. (CRSC)

Carrick Castle passing one of the Clyde shipyards with a distinctive longitudinal crane over the building berths. In 1881 she was sold to owners on the Firth of Forth, operating out of Leith, serving there for four seasons, and was sold in 1885 to A. Payne of Hastings for excursions from there. In 1888 she was purchased by Edwards, Robertson & Co. of Cardiff and renamed *Lady Margaret* for excursion service out of Cardiff and in 1895 became *Lord Tregedar*. In that year John Gunn purchased the Edwards, Robertson fleet and she was scrapped shortly afterwards. (G.E. Langmuir collection, Mitchell Library)

Windsor Castle was built in 1875 by T.B. Seath of Rutherglen, with single diagonal machinery by W. King & Co. Originally flush-decked, within a few years she was fitted with a narrow aft deck-saloon, as seen here at Lochgoilhead. Later she was fitted with a full-width fore saloon.

Windsor Castle at Douglas Pier, across the loch from Lochgoilhead. She was withdrawn in 1900 and sold to Turkish owners. She was renamed *Eser-i Sevket* and served until she was scrapped in 1918. McQueen's claim that she was used to convey the Sultan's harem across to the Asian shore is apocryphal.

The final steamer to be built for the Lochgoil Co. was *Edinburgh Castle*, built by R. Duncan of Port Glasgow, with single-cylinder diagonal machinery by Rankin & Blackmore, in 1879. She is seen here passing the cargo steamer *Bute 4* in the river. *Edinburgh Castle* was noted for her extremely large paddle boxes. (CRSC)

SATURDAY EXCURSION.

KILCREGGAN AND DUNOON

BY

WINDSOR CASTLE,

at 8.30 A.M.,

Calling at PARTICK and GOVAN, thence direct to KILCREGGAN and DUNOON. Returning from Dunoon by LORD OF THE ISLES at 6.10 P.M., and from Kilcreggan by EDINBURGH CASTLE at 5.15 P.M.

RETURN FARES:—Saloon, 1s 6d; Steerage, 1s.

M. T. CLARK, 5 Oswald Street.

NOTICE.—Passengers leaving Glasgow by Benmore at 2 P.M. for Dunoon, can return by Lord of the Isles at 6.10 P.M.

INVERARAY AND OBAN. FAMED LOCH ECK TOUR,

BY

LORD OF THE ISLES.

From Glasgow (Bridge Wharf), at 7.20 A.M. Trains—Central, 8.45 A.M.; St Enoch's, 8.30 A.M.; Queen Street, 8.0 A.M. (Join at Dunoon) for INVERARAY. Returning at 2.30 P.M. for Gourock, Prince's Pier, and Glasgow.

OBSERVE.—About 1 Hour on Land at Inveraray, 1½ Hours Strachur, 2 Hours Crarae.

RETURN FARES—Available for Season.

Dunoon	2/	1/6	Kyles of Bute	3/6	2/6
Rothesay	2/6	1/6	Inveraray	6/	3/6

Loch Eck Tour, 11/.

M. T. CLARK, 5 Oswald Street.

LOCHGOILHEAD & ARROCHAR,

BY

Saloon Steamers EDINBURGH CASTLE and WINDSOR CASTLE—

	Trains	
At 9 A.M. Daily	Central....	10 A.M.
	St Enoch..	10.5 ,,
At 10 ,, Daily ex. Sats ..	Central....	11.0 ,,
	St Enoch..	11.5 ,,

Via KILCREGGAN, COVE, and BLAIRMORE.

Returning from Lochgoilhead at 1.40 P.M. ex. Sats.; 4 P.M. Daily, and 6.30 P.M. Sats. only; Arrochar, 3 P.M.

To Arrochar, per 9 A.M. Steamer, Daily ex. Sats. Change Steamers at Princes Pier.

OBSERVE CHEAP FARES AND DINING.

Day's Sail,	Lochgoilhead	Saloon	2/	Steerage	1/
Do.	Do. and Dinner	,,	3/6	,,	2/
Do.	Do. Dinner & Tea	,,	4/3	,,	2/6
Do.	Arrochar	,,	2/6	,,	1/6

M. T. CLARK, 5 Oswald Street.

An undated newspaper advertisement, probably from the 1890s, showing a day excursion to Kilcreggan and Dunoon by *Windsor Castle*, returning by *Edinburgh Castle* or *Lord of the Isles*; the Inveraray service of *Lord of the Isles*; the Lochgoilhead and Arrochar services of *Edinburgh Castle* and *Windsor Castle*, offering a twice-daily service to these piers.

Above: Edinburgh Castle at Lochgoilhead. She passed to the merged Lochgoil & Inveraray Co. in 1909 and to Turbine Steamers Ltd in 1912, and was sold for scrapping in November 1913. (A. Ernest Glen collection)

After *Edinburgh Castle* was withdrawn, MacBrayne took over the Lochgoilhead service briefly with *Chevalier*. July 1914 saw the purchase of *Ivanhoe* by Turbine Steamers Ltd, and she operated for them with deep black tops to the funnels contrasting with the thin black tops she had previously appeared in. She is seen here passing Erskine Ferry. She only served the Lochgoilhead route for one summer and the service was then taken over by MacBrayne's little motor vessel *Comet*. (For her full history, see *Caledonian Steam Packet Co. Ltd* (G.E. Langmuir collection, Mitchell Library)

Opposite below: In 1885 the Lochgoil Co. took over the 1880 *Chancellor*, seen here off Greenock, from the Lochlomond Steamboat Co. She operated from Helensburgh and Greenock to Arrochar, with a connection to the Loch Lomond steamers there. In autumn 1891 she was sold to the GSWR. (For her full history, see *Glasgow and South Western and other Steamers.*)

Four
The Two Lords

In 1877 the Glasgow & Inveraray Steamboat Co. was formed. Malcolm T. Clark, manager of the Lochgoil company, was also its manager and secretary. A luxurious paddle steamer, *Lord of the Isles*, built by D. & W. Henderson, commenced this new service from Greenock, Dunoon and Wemyss Bay to Inveraray on 2 July of that year. This was the first day-return service offered to the Loch Fyne port. From 1881 she started from Glasgow in the peak months of July and August. In 1882 and then from 1885 onwards she did not call at Wemyss Bay. From the opening of Gourock Pier in 1889 calls were made there. (CRSC)

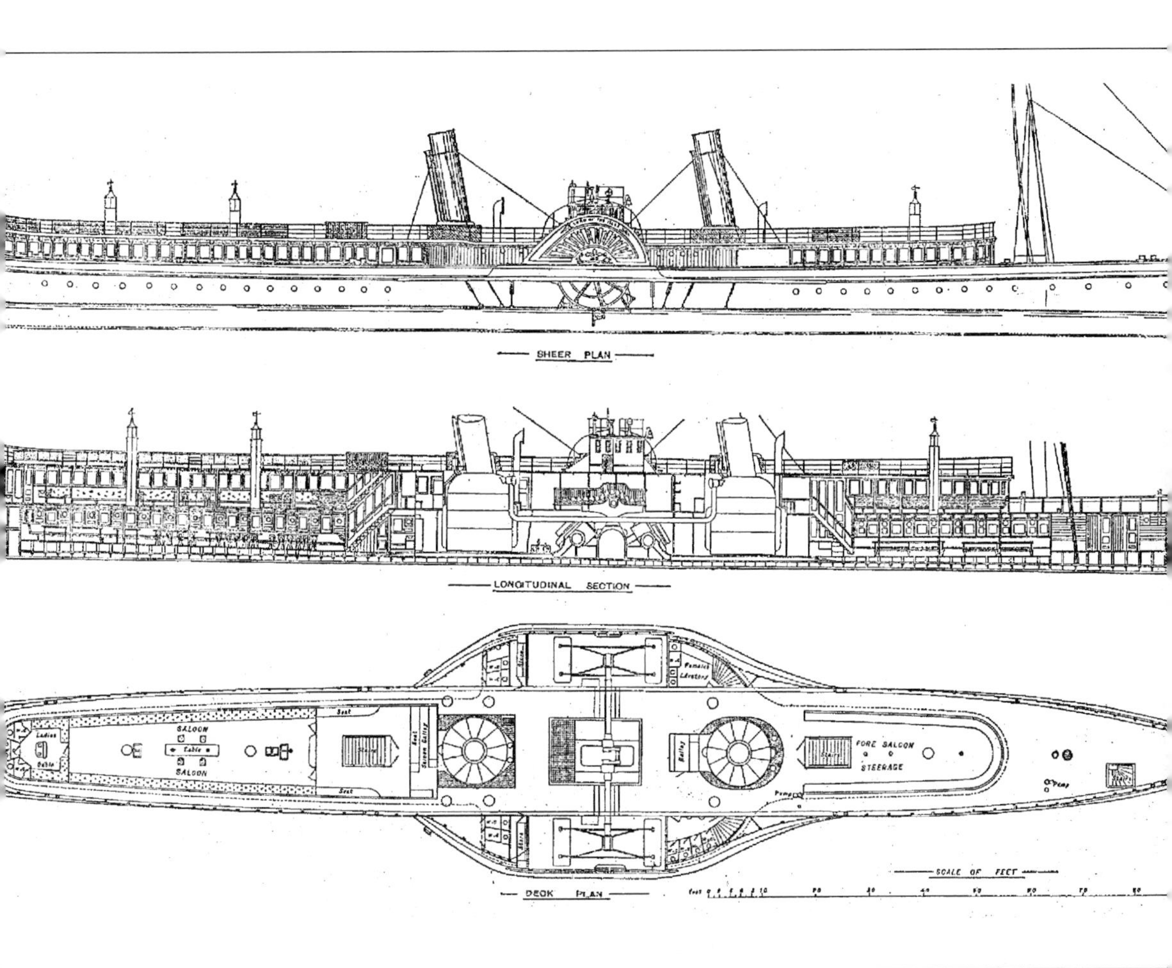

Plans for the first *Lord of the Isles*. Her deck saloons did not stretch to the edge of the hull and the seating around the edge of the aft saloon, rather than across it, was the result of this lack of breadth. (G.E. Langmuir collection, Mitchell Library)

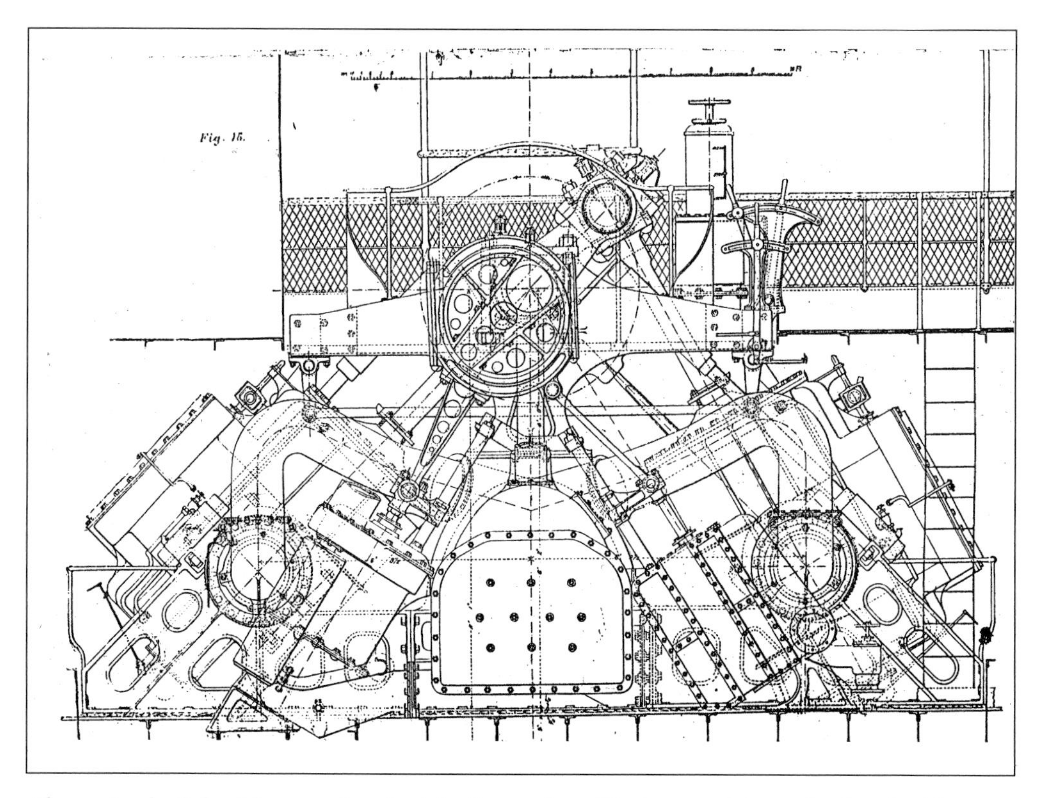

Above: Lord of the Isles was fitted with diagonal oscillating machinery by her builders, an unusual set-up as seen in this drawing. She was the first excursion steamer to be fitted with electric lighting. (G.E. Langmuir collection, Mitchell Library)

Opposite: In 1878 the steamer *Fairy Queen* entered service on Loch Eck, thus enabling the Lock Eck tour to commence. Passengers sailed to Kilmun by *Vivid*, by coach to Inverchapel, on *Fairy Queen* up Loch Eck, by coach to Strachur, and on *Lord of the Isles* to Inveraray and back from there to Greenock. (G.E. Langmuir collection, Mitchell Library)

NEW ROUTES TO THE WEST HIGHLANDS.

GLASGOW,

INVERARAY AND OBAN,

Via Greenock, Wemyss Bay, and Kyles of Bute.

The Splendid Saloon Steamer

"LORD OF THE ISLES,"

(Speed 23 miles an hour),

SAILS DAILY from GREENOCK (Custom House Quay) at 8.15 a.m., Princes Pier at 8.30 a.m., for KIRN, DUNOON, WEMYSS BAY, ROTHESAY, KYLES OF BUTE, STRACHUR, and INVERARAY, connecting with the undernoted Trains at Greenock and Wemyss Bay:—

From GLASGOW (St Enoch), via Greenock (Princes Pier), ...at 7.25 a.m.
Do. (Central and Bridge St.), via Greenock,.......at 7.30 a.m.
Do. (Bridge St.), via Wemyss Bay,.................at 8.10 a.m.
From EDINBURGH (Princes Street), via Wemyss Bay,.........at 6.40 a.m.

Returning from Inveraray at 2 p.m., and Rothesay about 5.10 p.m., for Wemyss Bay, Dunoon, Kirn, and Greenock, for Special Trains leaving Wemyss Bay at 5.45 p.m., for Glasgow, Edinburgh, and the South, and Greenock (Princes Pier) at 6.25 p.m., and Cathcart Street at 6.35 p.m. for Glasgow and Edinburgh.

Coaches in connection to and from Inveraray and Dalmally for Oban

Passengers through this varied Picturesque and Magnificent Scenery can have about Two Hours Ashore at Strachur and One Hour at Inveraray, the ancient capital of Argyllshire

Fares—Return—	1st Class and Saloon.	2nd Class and Saloon.	3rd Class and Steerage.
Glasgow to Strachur or Inveraray, via Greenock or Wemyss Bay,.........	7s 6d.	6s. 6d.	5s.

Greenock to Strachur or Inveraray,......	Saloon,	5s. 6d.	Steerage,	3s. 6d.
Dunoon & W. Bay do. do.	Do.	4s. 6d.	Do.	3s. 0d.
Rothesay do. do.	Do.	4s. 0d.	Do.	2s. 6d.
Kyles of Bute do. do.	Do.	3s. 0d.	Do.	2s. 0d.

LOCH ECK ROUTE,

By Splendid Saloon Steamer "LORD OF THE ISLES," from Greenock at 8.15 a.m. to DUNOON (Train from Glasgow, St Enoch at 7.25 a.m. and Central at 7.30 a.m.); or Steamer "VIVID" to KILMUN—Train from Central at 8 a.m.; St Enoch at 8.10 a.m.; thence by COACHES to INVERCHAPEL, Steamer "FAIRY QUEEN" on LOCH ECK, COACHES to STRACHUR, STEAMER to INVERARAY, and COACHES to DALMALLY for OBAN; returning from Oban in July at 9.50 a.m., from Inveraray at 2.0 p.m., and from Strachur at 2.15 p.m., as above, for Greenock, Glasgow, Edinburgh, and the South.

Also by Steamer "IVANHOE" from Greenock at 9.55 a.m., for DUNOON (Train from Central at 9 a.m. and St Enoch at 8 55 a.m.); thence by COACHES from Dunoon and Kirn to INVERCHAPEL; Steamer "FAIRY QUEEN" on LOCH ECK, and COACHES to STRACHUR; returning from Strachur at 2.15 p.m., as above, for Greenock, Glasgow, Edinburgh, and the South.

For full particulars as to Circular Tours, Fares, etc., see Time Bills, to be had on board Steamers; at Railway Stations; from George Stirling, Jr., Dunoon; John Rodger, Inveraray; and from

M. T. CLARK, MANAGER,
17 Oswald Street, Glasgow.

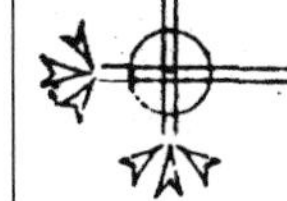

The first *Lord of the Isles* at the single berth pier at Dunoon. Her arrival on the scene caused David MacBrayne to order the magnificent *Columba* for the Royal Route from Glasgow to Ardrishaig.

Opposite below: The year 1891 saw the replacement of *Lord of the Isles* by her successor of the same name. The earlier steamer was sold to the Thames to the Victoria Steamboat Association. She retained her Lochgoil funnel colours and operated from London to Harwich. Before leaving the Clyde she had telescopic funnels fitted. Also while on the Thames her narrow after-deck saloon was replaced by a full width one. She is seen here, unusually, at St Paul's Wharf, with St Paul's Cathedral in the background, and with her forward funnel lowered. (Tom Lee collection)

Lord of the Isles met the challenge from *Columba* by being improved for the 1879 season. Her forward-deck saloon was brought forward almost to the mast, and her funnels were lengthened, thus keeping the aft deck clear of soot and smuts. Note the telescopic funnels, which were unique amongst Clyde steamers. (Douglas Brown collection)

From 1894 *Lord of the Isles* sailed from London Bridge to Southend and Margate, occasionally extending her sailings to Ramsgate. On 16 May 1894 she had a contretemps with London Bridge, losing both her funnels. After the 1896 season she was sold to Mrs C. Black and renamed *Jupiter*. This company went bankrupt in 1898 after ordering a new steamer from the Clydebank Shipbuilding & Engineering Co., which later became *Juno* of the GSWR. *Jupiter* was laid up and returned to the Clyde as *Lady of the Isles*. She is seen here, having just arrived back in the Clyde from the Thames under tow. Note the telescopic funnels. (CRSC)

Lady of the Isles approaching Dunoon. She ran excursions for A. Dawson Reid from Glasgow in 1903, in competition with the Buchanan steamers. On 29 August of that year she suffered boiler trouble off Greenock en route from Glasgow to Tighnabruaich and did not sail again. She lay at Bowling and was scrapped at Dumbarton in 1905.

The second *Lord of the Isles* was also built by D. & W. Henderson, entering service in the summer of 1891. She differed from her predecessor in that her deck saloons were carried out to the edge of the hull. She is seen here in Rothesay Bay in a G. Washington Wilson postcard view.

The second *Lord of the Isles* arriving at Rothesay in her early condition.

By the end of the 1890s, *Lord of the Isles* had had her promenade deck extended to the bow. She is seen here in that condition at Inveraray. The wooden T-shaped extension to the old stone jetty had been built for the first *Lord* at the time she entered service. (CRSC Archive)

The second *Lord* approaching Kames pier in the Kyles of Bute. (CRSC Archive)

Lord of the Isles, like *Columba*, had her own post office, although using a cachet rather than the special postmark of *Columba*, which was stamped on all mail posted on board.

All Round the Clock – a day on the *Lord of the Isles*, showing where and when the steamer would pass any points of interest and call at piers at each point of her journey on her 12¾ hour day. (CRSC Archive)

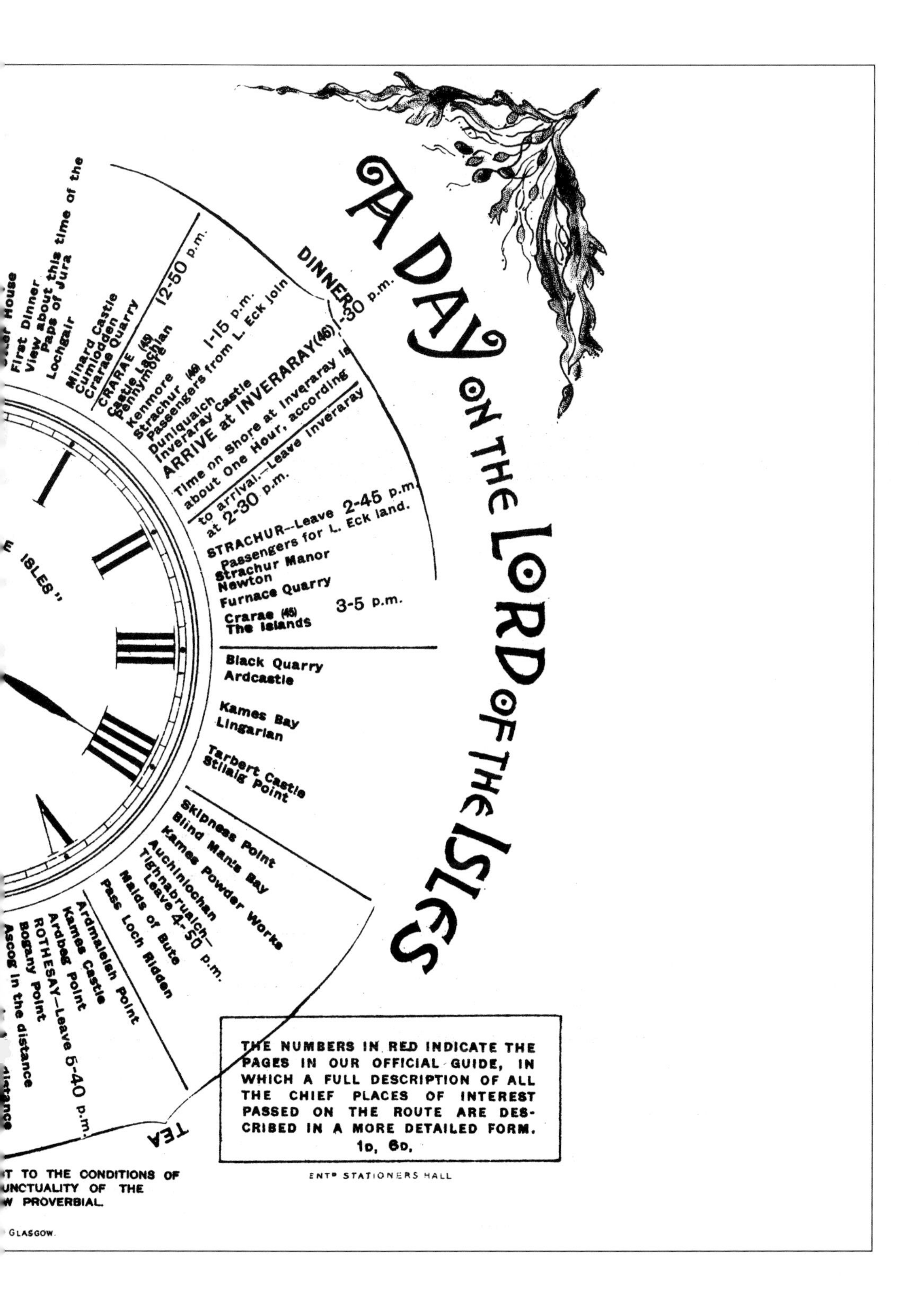

A DAY ON THE LORD OF THE ISLES
First Dinner
View about this time of the Paps of Jura
Lochgair
Minard Castle
Cumlodden
Crarae Quarry
12-50 p.m.
CRARAE (45)
Castle Lachlan
Pennymore
Kenmore
Strachur (46) 1-15 p.m.
Passengers from L. Eck join
Duniquaich
Inveraray Castle
ARRIVE at INVERARAY (46)
DINNER 1-30 p.m.
Time on Shore at Inveraray is about One Hour, according to arrival.—Leave Inveraray at 2-30 p.m.
STRACHUR—Leave 2-45 p.m.
Passengers for L. Eck land.
Strachur Manor
Newton
Furnace Quarry
Crarae (45) 3-5 p.m.
The Islands
Black Quarry
Ardcastle
Kames Bay
Lingarian
Tarbert Castle
Stilaig Point
Skipness Point
Blind Man's Bay
Kames Powder Works
Auchinlochan
Tighnabruaich—Leave 4-50 p.m.
Maids of Bute
Pass Loch Ridden
Ardmaleish Point
Kames Castle
Ardbeg Point
ROTHESAY—Leave 5-40 p.m.
Bogany Point
Ascog in the distance
TEA
THE NUMBERS IN RED INDICATE THE PAGES IN OUR OFFICIAL GUIDE, IN WHICH A FULL DESCRIPTION OF ALL THE CHIEF PLACES OF INTEREST PASSED ON THE ROUTE ARE DESCRIBED IN A MORE DETAILED FORM. 1D, 6D.
ENTD STATIONERS HALL
T TO THE CONDITIONS OF
UNCTUALITY OF THE
W PROVERBIAL.
GLASGOW.

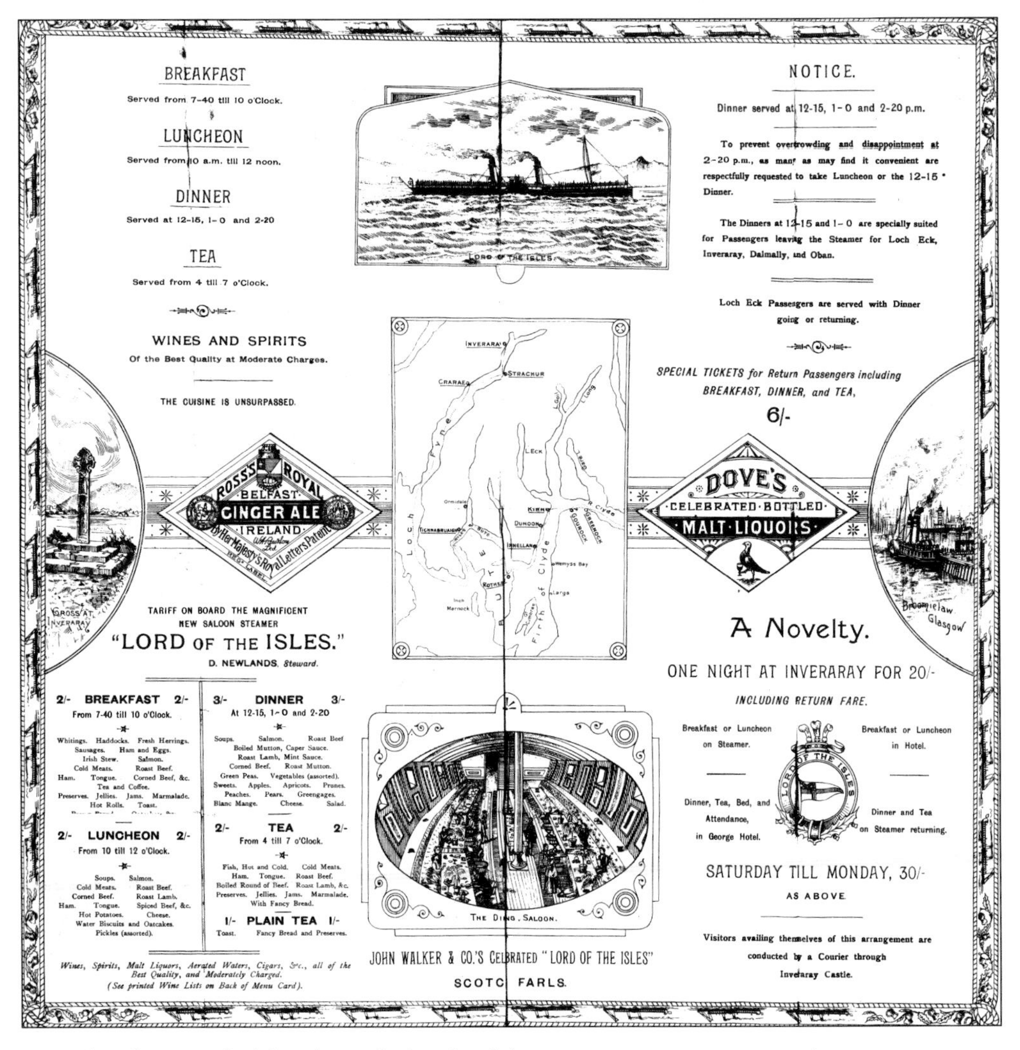

A napkin from *Lord of the Isles* with details of the catering arrangements and menus.

Lord of the Isles arriving at a pier.

An official company postcard of Loch Eck with a vignette of *Lord of the Isles* in the top left-hand corner.

Above: Lord of the Isles seen dressed overall in an 'On Board' postcard. (CRSC Archive)

Opposite: Following the takeover by Turbine Steamers Ltd, *Lord of the Isles* was placed on a Round Bute cruise from the Broomielaw, as featured in this series of advertisements for 1912. They also included *King Edward* to Inveraray, *Queen Alexandra* to Campbeltown, *Edinburgh Castle* to *Lochgoilhead* and *Kylemore* and *Benmore* to the Comet Centenary Review. (G.E. Langmuir collection, Mitchell Library)

Left: Lord of the Isles continued to sail from Glasgow during the First World War, mainly to Lochgoilhead. In 1919 she reverted to sailing to the Kyles of Bute and from 1920, round Bute. Left is a cartoon from the *Evening Times* of Friday 20 June 1919, following the end of a stoker's strike. (G.E. Langmuir collection, Mitchell Library)

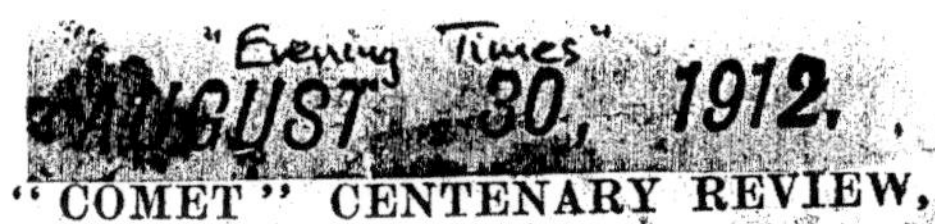

"COMET" CENTENARY REVIEW,
31st AUGUST.

Passengers per TURBINE STEAMERS to INVERARAY or CAMPBELTOWN may on Return Journey Travel via Princes Pier and obtain an Excellent View of the Representative FLEET at the TAIL OF THE BANK.
Return portion of Campbeltown Tickets, via Wemyss Bay or Fairlie, are Valid to Return via Greenock (Princes Pier).

INVERARAY, Via KYLES OF BUTE.
AND THE
FAMED LOCH ECK TOUR.
By the Fast and Luxurious Turbine
"KING EDWARD"

Daily about 9 a.m. from Prince's Pier.
Trains—St Enoch 8.20 a.m., Central 8.20 a.m., Queen St. 8.5 a.m. (join at Dunoon), Steamer from Gourock 9.10 a.m., Dunoon 9.30, Rothesay 10.15, thence to Tighnabruaich, Crarae, Strachur, and Inveraray. Returning from Inveraray at 2.15 p.m., arriving Glasgow by rail 7.30 p.m.
Return Day Fares:—3rd and Sal., 6/-; 3rd & Stge., 5/-.
Valid During Season:—3rd & Sal., 7/-; 3rd & Stge., 5/6.
Loch Eck Tour, 3rd and Cabin, 11s 6d.

CAMPBELTOWN
(Via West of Arran),
By NEW TURBINE STEAMER
"QUEEN ALEXANDRA."

Trains—Central, 8.55 a.m. to Wemyss Bay; St Enoch, 9.20 to Fairlie; Queen St., 8.5 (join at Dunoon). Steamer from Prince's Pier 8.45 a.m., Gourock 9.5, Dunoon 9.28, Wemyss Bay 9.50, Fairlie 10.25, thence to Lochranza, Pirnmill, Machrie Bay, and Campbeltown. Returning from Campbeltown at 2.50 p.m., arriving Glasgow by Rail 6.45 p.m.
Light Railway in connection for MACHRIHANISH, ON THE SHORES OF THE ATLANTIC.
Return Day Fares:—3rd & Sal., 6/; 3rd & Stge., 5/
Valid During Season:—3rd & Sal., 7/; 3rd & Stge., 5/6

CLOSING
MOONLIGHT CRUISE
(Weather Favourable)

TO-NIGHT (FRIDAY), 30th AUGUST.—TO GRAND ILLUMINATION AND FIREWORK DISPLAY AT DUNOON AND ROTHESAY.
Trains in connection with above Cruise leave Glasgow, St Enoch, 6.5 p.m.; Central, 6.25 p.m. Passengers booking from St Enoch return via Gourock.
RETURN FARES (Rail and Steamer):—
1st and Saloon, 3s; 3rd and Saloon, 2s.
JOHN WILLIAMSON, 99 Gt. Clyde Street, Glasgow.

TRADES' HOLIDAY
AND
"COMET" CENTENARY REVIEW,
TO-MORROW (SATURDAY), 31st AUGUST.
NOTE.—NO RETURN TICKETS Issued to DUNOON TO-MORROW (SATURDAY), 31st AUGUST.

NEW EXCURSION ROUTE.
FROM GLASGOW (BRIDGE WHARF), DAILY
(Except Sundays),
By the Magnificent Saloon Steamer
"LORD OF THE ISLES,"
AT 11.30 A.M.

(Train—Central, 12.15 p.m. to Gourock).
Calling at GOVAN 11.40 a.m., RENFREW 12 Noon. From PRINCE'S PIER 1.15 p.m., GOUROCK 1.30, DUNOON 1.45, ROTHESAY 2.40, TIGHNABRUAICH 3.20, KAMES 3.25.
Thence ROUND THE
ISLAND OF BUTE.
Returning from Rothesay at 5.40 p.m., Dunoon 6.15 p.m., arriving Glasgow about 8.30 p.m.
RETURN FARES by Steamer from Glasgow.

	Sal.	F. Sal.		Sal.	F. Sal.
Dunoon	1/6	1/	Rothesay	2/-	1/6
Kyles of Bute	3/-	2/6	Round Bute ...	3/-	2/6

Day's Sail (Saloon), with Dinner and Plain Tea, 5s.
Rail and Steamer.
Round Bute—3rd and Sal., 4/6; 3rd and Stge., 3/9.
Passengers returning from Kyles take "Columba" or "King Edward" from Tighnabruaich.

To LOCHGOIL,
"EDINBURGH CASTLE,"
FROM GLASGOW (BRIDGE WHARF) DAILY,
AT 9 A.M.

Trains—St Enoch, 10.5 a.m.; Central, 10.10 a.m.
Returning from Lochgoilhead at 4 p.m.
Arriving Glasgow about 7.45 p.m.
Return Day Fares ....Saloon, 2s; Steerage, 1s 6d.
Valid during Season ......Saloon, 2s 6d; Steerage, 2s.
Day's Sail (Saloon) with Dinner and Tea, 4s 6d.
Drive to Ardgoil Estate, 1s.
JOHN WILLIAMSON, 99 Gt. Clyde Street, Glasgow.

TRADES' HOLIDAY.
"COMET" CENTENARY REVIEW,
SATURDAY, 31st AUGUST.
Magnificent Saloon Steamer
"KYLEMORE"
Will Sail from GLASGOW (BRIDGE WHARF),
At 1.30 p.m.,
TO DUNOON AND ROTHESAY,
Calling at GOVAN and RENFREW.
Returning from Rothesay at 6.30 p.m., Dunoon, 7.10 p.m.
RETURN FARES—Saloon, 2s; Fore-Saloon, 1s 6d.
JOHN WILLIAMSON, 99 Gt. Clyde Street, Glasgow.

TRADES' HOLIDAY.
31st AUGUST, 1912.
"COMET" CELEBRATIONS
AND
WARSHIPS
At the TAIL OF THE BANK.
Saloon Steamer
"BENMORE"
Will Sail from
GLASGOW (BRIDGE WHARF),
At 2.30 p.m.

Calling at GOVAN and RENFREW. Round the Great Fleet of Representative Vessels at the Tail of the Bank, affording passengers an excellent view, and proceeding to DUNOON, allowing 1 hour on shore.
Returning from Dunoon, 6.30 p.m.
RETURN FARE, 1s 6d.
JOHN WILLIAMSON, 99 Great Clyde St., Glasgow.

Lord of the Isles did not sail in 1926, her fitting out being affected by the General Strike, but she was back on the Round Bute cruise in 1927. In 1928, she was placed on the Lochgoilhead and Arrochar service, replacing *Iona*. In that year she spent a short time in the spring on the Ardrishaig Mail service. She is seen here at Lochgoilhead. (CRSC)

These out-of-the-ordinary trips in 1928 were to be the swansong of *Lord of the Isles*. She was broken up at the end of that year by Smith & Co. at Port Glasgow.

Five

White Funnel Turbines

The experimental turbine launch *Turbinia* had been built on Tyneside in 1894 as a showpiece for the marine steam turbine engine invented by Charles Parsons. On 26 June 1897 she demonstrated her speed as an unofficial participant at the Diamond Jubilee Fleet Review at Spithead. She raced along the lines of warships at a speed of 34 1/2 knots. Parsons founded the Parsons Marine Steam Turbine Co. Ltd, and turbines were installed in a couple of torpedo-boat destroyers, which entered service in 1900-1901: *HMS Viper* and *HMS Cobra*. The former was lost on 3 August 1901 after striking rocks off Alderney and on 18 September of that year *Cobra* broke in two and sank off the Lincolnshire coast on her delivery voyage from the Tyne.

King Edward, when launched in 1901, was not only the first Clyde steamer to have turbine propulsion, but also the very first commercial turbine-powered steamer in the world. She was initially owned by the Turbine Steamer Syndicate, which involved John Williamson, the Parsons Marine Steam Turbine Co., and William Denny & Bros. Ltd, shipbuilders, of Dumbarton. This syndicate was formed in January 1901.

King Edward was named following a competition amongst the general public with a prize of £5, which was shared amongst fifteen competitors who had suggested that name. She was launched on 16 May, and ran trials from 14 June, with a speed of 19.7 knots being reached. On 28 June she had a demonstration run to Lochranza and Campbeltown with specially invited VIP passengers, and is seen here on that sailing.

King Edward entered service on 1 July 1901 from Greenock Princes Pier, Dunoon, Rothesay and Fairlie to Lochranza and Campbeltown, replacing *Strathmore* on that route.

King Edward arriving at Campbeltown with large crowds, both on the steamer and on the pier. She continued to give an Easter Monday cruise to Campbeltown until 1911, after she had moved to the Inveraray route.

King Edward, seen here leaving Tarbert, had three propeller shafts, originally with a total of five screws, two on each of the two outer shafts and one on the central one. In 1905 this was reduced to three, with only one on each of the outer shafts. The hull was a copy of that of the paddler *Duchess of Hamilton*, and *King Edward* was designed to be converted to paddle if the turbine experiment was not successful, In fact, until 1935, marks could be seen on her deck planking where sponsons were to be fitted in the event of this conversion taking place. But all went well with the turbines and she was the precursor of many turbine steamers, including cross-channel steamers, ocean liners, cargo ships and tankers that were to be built over the next sixty and more years.

In 1902, following the debut of *Queen Alexandra*, *King Edward* was transferred to a new route to Ardrishaig, competing with *Columba*. In that summer only she called at Tarbert, where she is seen here.

King Edward arriving at Ardrishaig in a postcard view. (CRSC slide collection)

King Edward at Ardrishaig. On 1 September 1902 a new company, Turbine Steamers Ltd, was formed to take over from the Syndicate.

From 1903 *King Edward* extended her sailings to Inveraray, and the calls at Tarbert ceased. She now called at Gourock, Wemyss Bay, and Fairlie, but not at Rothesay, sailing via Garroch Head. She now competed with *Lord of the Isles* for the Inveraray traffic as well as with *Columba* for the Ardrishaig traffic.

From her first season, *King Edward* offered evening cruises on the firth, including sailings from Helensburgh from 1904.

In 1906, *King Edward* was fitted with an upper deck and the lifeboats were relocated to the aft end of this deck. She is seen here approaching Dunoon in that condition.

An illustration from an official Turbine Steamers guidebook of around 1912, showing part of the machinery of *King Edward*.

The dining saloon of *King Edward* or *Queen Alexandra* from the same guidebook.

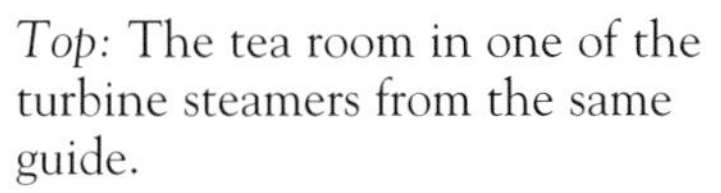

Top: The tea room in one of the turbine steamers from the same guide.

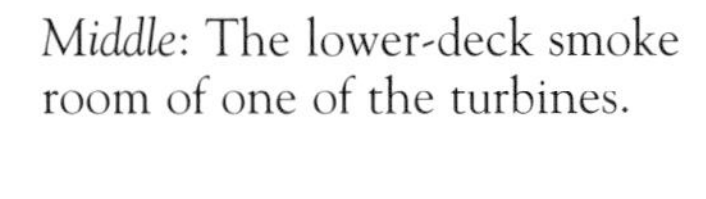

Middle: The lower-deck smoke room of one of the turbines.

Below: King Edward at Inveraray. In some seasons only fifteen minutes ashore was given here.

A well-filled *King Edward* about to depart from Inveraray after 1906. From 1909 the Tighnabruaich call was withdrawn, and seventy-five minutes were now being given ashore at Inveraray. From 1909 to 1911 a cruise up Loch Fyne to off Dunderave Castle and Cairndow was offered during this time. The Fairlie call had been withdrawn by this time and the steamer operated via the Kyles of Bute with calls at Tighnabruaich and Strachur. From 1911 the Wemyss Bay call was no longer made. (CRSC archive)

King Edward, *Lord of the Isles* and *Duchess of Fife* at Rothesay. In March 1912 Turbine Steamers Ltd purchased the Lochgoil & Inveraray Steamboat Co., competition from the turbine having proved too much for the paddler.

On 2 February 1915, *King Edward* left the Clyde for war service. She served as a troopship from Southampton to Le Havre and Rouen. In 1919 King Edward was used as a hospital ship in the Archangel campaign, in support of the White Russians. On 28 September she was the last non-naval vessel to leave the port. She was almost lost in a severe storm on her way back across the North Sea. She is seen here at Oban on 2 December 1919 on the final leg of her journey back from war. The structure on the foredeck was part of the hospital accommodation.

In 1920 *King Edward* returned to the Campbeltown route, which she maintained until replaced by *King George V* in 1927. She is seen here departing Rothesay. (CRSC Archive)

An excursion could be made on the narrow gauge Campbeltown & Macrihanish Railway to Macrihanish 'on the shores of the Atlantic', giving seventy-five minutes there.

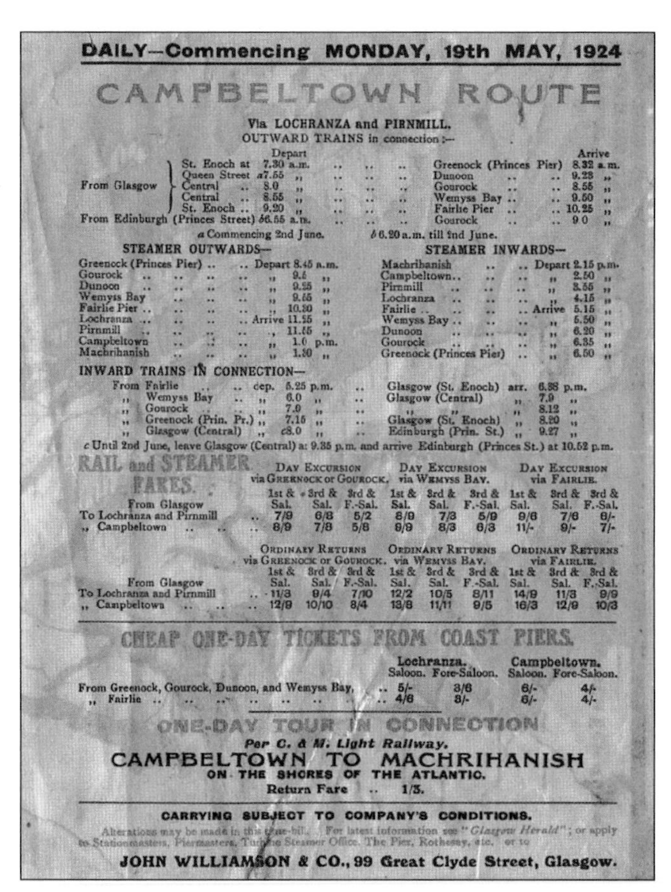

DAILY—Commencing MONDAY, 19th MAY, 1924

CAMPBELTOWN ROUTE

Via LOCHRANZA and PIRNMILL.

OUTWARD TRAINS in connection :—

	Depart		Arrive
From Glasgow St. Enoch at	7.30 a.m.	Greenock (Princes Pier)	8.32 a.m.
Queen Street	a7.55 "	Dunoon	9.28 "
Central	8.0 "	Gourock	8.55 "
Central	8.55 "	Wemyss Bay	9.50 "
St. Enoch	9.20 "	Fairlie Pier	10.25 "
From Edinburgh (Princes Street)	b6.55 a.m.	Gourock	9 0 "

a Commencing 2nd June. b 6.20 a.m. till 2nd June.

STEAMER OUTWARDS—		STEAMER INWARDS—	
Greenock (Princes Pier)	Depart 8.45 a.m.	Machrihanish	Depart 2.15 p.m.
Gourock	" 9.5 "	Campbeltown	" 2.50 "
Dunoon	" 9.25 "	Pirnmill	" 3.55 "
Wemyss Bay	" 9.55 "	Lochranza	" 4.15 "
Fairlie Pier	" 10.30 "	Fairlie	Arrive 5.15 "
Lochranza	Arrive 11.55 "	Wemyss Bay	" 5.50 "
Pirnmill	" 11.55 "	Dunoon	" 6.20 "
Campbeltown	" 1.0 p.m.	Gourock	" 6.35 "
Machrihanish	" 1.30 "	Greenock (Princes Pier)	" 6.50 "

INWARD TRAINS IN CONNECTION—

From Fairlie	dep. 5.25 p.m.	Glasgow (St. Enoch)	arr. 6.38 p.m.
" Wemyss Bay	" 6.0 "	Glasgow (Central)	" 7.9 "
" Gourock	" 7.0 "	" "	" 8.12 "
" Greenock (Prin. Pr.)	" 7.15 "	Glasgow (St. Enoch)	" 8.20 "
" Glasgow (Central)	" c8.0 "	Edinburgh (Prin. St.)	" 9.27 "

c Until 2nd June, leave Glasgow (Central) at 9.35 p.m. and arrive Edinburgh (Princes St.) at 10.52 p.m.

RAIL and STEAMER FARES.

From Glasgow	Day Excursion via Greenock or Gourock. 1st & Sal.	3rd & Sal.	3rd & F.-Sal.	Day Excursion via Wemyss Bay. 1st & Sal.	3rd & Sal.	3rd & F.-Sal.	Day Excursion via Fairlie. 1st & Sal.	3rd & Sal.	3rd & F.-Sal.
To Lochranza and Pirnmill	7/9	6/8	5/2	8/9	7/3	5/9	9/6	7/6	6/-
" Campbeltown	8/9	7/8	5/8	9/9	8/3	6/3	11/-	9/-	7/-

From Glasgow	Ordinary Returns via Greenock or Gourock. 1st & Sal.	3rd & Sal.	3rd & F.-Sal.	Ordinary Returns via Wemyss Bay. 1st & Sal.	3rd & Sal.	3rd & F.-Sal.	Ordinary Returns via Fairlie. 1st & Sal.	3rd & Sal.	3rd & F.-Sal.
To Lochranza and Pirnmill	11/3	9/4	7/10	12/2	10/5	8/11	14/9	11/3	9/9
" Campbeltown	12/9	10/10	8/4	13/8	11/11	9/5	16/3	12/9	10/3

CHEAP ONE-DAY TICKETS FROM COAST PIERS.

	Lochranza. Saloon.	Fore-Saloon.	Campbeltown. Saloon.	Fore-Saloon.
From Greenock, Gourock, Dunoon, and Wemyss Bay,	5/-	3/6	6/-	4/-
" Fairlie	4/6	3/-	6/-	4/-

ONE-DAY TOUR IN CONNECTION

Per C. & M. Light Railway.

CAMPBELTOWN TO MACHRIHANISH

ON THE SHORES OF THE ATLANTIC.

Return Fare .. 1/3.

CARRYING SUBJECT TO COMPANY'S CONDITIONS.

Alterations may be made in this time-bill. For latest information see *"Glasgow Herald"*; or apply to Stationmasters, Piermasters, Turbine Steamer Office, The Pier, Rothesay, etc. or to

JOHN WILLIAMSON & CO., 99 Great Clyde Street, Glasgow.

Above: The 1924 timetable for sailings to Campbeltown by *King Edward*. (Tom Lee collection)

Right: From 1928 onwards *King Edward* offered occasional excursions to Stranraer, as seen in this handbill from 1934. (CRSC archive)

NEW

SPECIAL EXCURSION

(WEATHER FAVOURABLE)

On FRIDAY, 10th AUGUST

BY TURBINE STEAMER

"King Edward"

— TO —

STRANRAER

(Allowing about 1 hour on Shore)

From	Depart	Due back
HELENSBURGH	8-30 a.m.	8-20 p.m.
GOUROCK	8-40 a.m.	8-5 p.m.
DUNOON	9-0 a.m.	7-50 p.m.

Stranraer arrive 1-45 p.m.

Passengers will have an excellent view of BUTE, CUMBRAE, ARRAN, AILSA CRAIG, the AYRSHIRE and GALLOWAY COAST and LOCH RYAN

CHEAP DAY FARES:

Saloon 6/-; Fore-Saloon 4/-

John Williamson & Co., 308 Clyde Street, Glasgow, C.1.

King Edward with the royal yacht *Victoria and Albert* in an early aerial photograph. (CRSC archive).

In 1927 *King Edward* was transferred to Williamson-Buchanan Steamers Ltd, and sailed from the Broomielaw on the 13:30 to Rothesay and Loch Riddon. From 1929 onwards she sailed from Bridge Wharf on the south side of the river, as seen here.

SUNDAY
PLEASURE SAILS

From GLASGOW (Broomielaw) to

DUNOON, ROTHESAY
KYLES OF BUTE
AND
ARRAN CRUISES

LUXURIOUS STEAMERS
"KING EDWARD" (Turbine) - at 10-30 a.m.
"EAGLE" (or other Steamer) - at 11-0 a.m.
Calling at GOVAN, DUNOON and ROTHESAY

"KING EDWARD" will proceed from Rothesay at 2-20 p.m. on a Cruise along the shores of Arran, round Bute, etc., and is due back Glasgow at 8-0 p m.

"EAGLE" will call at Bowling, Greenock, Dunoon, and leave Rothesay at 2-25 p.m. on a Cruise through the far-famed Kyles of Bute. Due back Glasgow at 7-45 p.m.

Steamers return from Rothesay at 4-40 p.m. and 5-0 p.m.; Dunoon 5-20 p.m. and 5-40 p.m.

Passengers can have about 4 hours ashore at Rothesay or 5 hours at Dunoon.

CHEAP RETURN FARES FROM GLASGOW:

	SALOON	FORE-SALOON	SALOON with DINNER and PLAIN TEA	SALOON with DINNER and HIGH TEA
DUNOON -	3/6	2/6	—	—
ROTHESAY -	4/-	3/-	8/6	9/6
DAY'S SAIL	5/-	4/-	9/6	10/6

NOTE:—For Special Sunday Afternoon Cruise at 2-15 p.m. from Glasgow,
SEE SEPARATE POSTER

JOHN WILLIAMSON & CO., 99 Great Clyde Street, Glasgow, C.1.

A handbill from 1927 or 1928 for Sunday cruises by *King Edward* and *Eagle III* from Glasgow (Broomielaw). (CRSC Archive)

SUNDAY CRUISES
By WHITE FUNNEL STEAMERS

LUXURIOUS TURBINE
"KING EDWARD"
From DUNOON at 12-40 p.m. Due back 5-40 p.m.
To ROTHESAY (where Passengers have some time on shore), thence cruising from ROTHESAY at 2-20 p.m., as under:—

AUGUST 7 - - - To BRODICK BAY (ARRAN)
" 14 - - - To GLEN SANNOX (ARRAN)
(Going via KYLES OF BUTE and returning via GARROCHHEAD)
" 21 - - - To HOLY ISLE (LAMLASH)
" 28 - - - ROUND BUTE and CUMBRAE
SEPTEMBER 4 - - To CORRIE (ARRAN)
(Going via KYLES OF BUTE and returning via GARROCHHEAD)

SALOON STEAMER
"EAGLE"
(Or Other Steamer)
From DUNOON at 1-20 p.m. Due back 5-20 p.m.
For ROTHESAY and Cruise through Far-Famed KYLES OF BUTE

MAGNIFICENT STEAMER
"QUEEN-EMPRESS"
(Or Other Steamer)
From DUNOON at 4-30 p.m. Due back 6-35 p.m.
For CRUISE to beautiful
LOCH LONG and LOCH GOIL

CHEAP AFTERNOON FARES FROM DUNOON:—

"KING EDWARD" CRUISE -	Saloon	3/-
"EAGLE" CRUISE - - - -	Do.	2/-
"QUEEN-EMPRESS" CRUISE	Do.	1/-

NOTE:—On SUNDAYS Steamers leave DUNOON for GLASGOW (Broomielaw) at 5-20 p.m., 5-40 p.m., 6-45 p.m.

JOHN WILLIAMSON & CO., 99 Great Clyde Street, Glasgow, C.1

A handbill for Sunday afternoon cruises from Dunoon in August 1932 by *King Edward*, *Eagle III*, and *Queen Empress*. (CRSC Archive)

Above: King Edward off Toward in 1932. By this time she was firmly ensconced on the 10:00 sailing from Glasgow to the Arran Coast. (Douglas McGowan collection)

Right: A 1934 handbill for upriver trips from Dunoon and Rothesay to see the Cunarder 534 (later *Queen Mary*) under construction. (CRSC archive)

DO NOT LEAVE THE CLYDE
WITHOUT SEEING

NO. 534

The Great New Cunarder building at Clydebank, due to be launched on 26th Sept. by Her Majesty the Queen

WHITE FUNNEL STEAMERS

SAIL DAILY UP THE RIVER TO

GLASGOW

From ROTHESAY	From DUNOON
[C] 8-15 a.m.	[C] 9-10 a.m.
[A] 3-45 p.m.	[A] 4-30 p.m.
4-40 p.m.	5-20 p.m.
[A] 5-30 p.m.	[A] 6-0 p.m.
[B] 6-15 p.m.	[B] 6-45 p.m.

A.—August Only B.—Saturdays Only
C.—Except Saturdays.

Affording an excellent view of the 73,000 ton Liner and the world-famous Clyde Shipyards.

SINGLE TICKETS TO GLASGOW FROM

Rothesay - - 2/6 or 1/9
Dunoon - - 2/- or 1/3

RETURN TICKETS ALSO ISSUED.

Tourists continue their journey from Glasgow

John Williamson & Co., 308 Clyde Street, Glasgow, C.1

King Edward at Lochgoilhead. From 1928 onwards a series of annual charters to Glasgow Corporation took the city's deprived schoolchildren from Glasgow to Lochgoilhead. These took about twelve days each year, with a total of 20,000 children being carried. From 1933 to 1939 she offered a Sunday afternoon cruise from Glasgow to Lochgoilhead.

King Edward, *Queen Mary*, and *Queen Alexandra* in winter lay-up in Greenock's Albert Harbour between 1933 and 1935. (CRSC)

The railway takeover in late 1935 saw little difference to *King Edward*'s activity. She is seen here with the CSP motor vessel *Ashton*. At this time she had a Class 5 certificate for 1966 and seems almost full here.

King Edward spent the war years from 1939 to 1945 in Clyde service, serving as a tender to the many troopships at the Tail of the Bank, and on the Gourock to Dunoon service. On 21 October 1941 she was in a collision with Burns Laird's *Lairdsburn* off Gourock. She is seen here after that event.

King Edward resumed peacetime sailings in 1946, now with yellow CSP funnels replacing the white funnels she had carried since building. On 1 June she resumed her Bridge Wharf sailings, taking the 11:00 to the Kyles of Bute. In 1948, in common with the remainder of the fleet, she was fitted with a wheelhouse and is seen in that condition in 1951 passing Stephen's yard at Linthouse with a damaged bow, the result of a collision with the puffer *Trojan* off Meadowside Granary. (Douglas McGowan collection)

King Edward at Ayr in the winter of 1950-51, where she received her final overhaul on what was the only time she visited the port. (CRSC)

King Edward arriving at Innellan post-1948. She was withdrawn after the 1951 season and sold for breaking up at Troon in June 1952. Two of her turbines were preserved for many years in Kelvingrove Art Gallery and Museum and are now in the Scottish Maritime Museum at Troon.

John Williamson lost no time in ordering a second turbine steamer for the Turbine Steamers Syndicate following the success of *King Edward* in her first season. *Queen Alexandra* was built in 1902, again by Denny's of Dumbarton, and took over the Campbeltown service from her predecessor. She is seen here off Fairlie in 1902 in original condition with her bridge only a few feet above the upper deck. (CRSC)

Following protests by passengers that they could not see forwards, John Williamson had the bridge raised by a few feet to give a forward view as in this postcard view.

In September 1902 *Queen Alexandra* made a week-long visit to Oban and is seen here berthed in Oban Bay amongst a plethora of steam yachts. Note Alexander Paterson's small screw steamer *Princess Louise* departing.

Queen Alexandra (1902) in the Sound of Kerrera on the occasion of her Oban visit.

Queen Alexandra (1902) at Lochranza. She was 20 feet longer and about a knot faster than her predecessor, and had the upper, or shade deck, from building.

Queen Alexandra (1902) arriving at Campbeltown in a postcard view. (CRSC archive)

Queen Alexandra (1902) berthed across the end of the pier at Campbeltown in another postcard view.

The Campbeltown service involved a ferry call at Pirnmill, as seen in this illustration from a turbine steamers guidebook.

Queen Alexandra (1902) on her return journey from Campbeltown at Lochranza.

On 10 September 1911 *Queen Alexandra* was seriously damaged by fire whilst laid up in the Albert Harbour at Greenock. She was sold to the Canadian Pacific Railway and rebuilt for service in British Columbia from Vancouver to Nanaimo as *Princess Patricia.* (CRSC)

Princess Patricia arriving at Vancouver on 20 August 1928. (Albert H. Paull, Robert Turner collection)

Princess Patricia was popular on the route and remained in service until 1928, when the car-carrying steamer *Princess Elaine* replaced her. She continued on relief sailings and excursions until scrapped in 1937.

Princess Patricia in the process of being scrapped in 1937. Note the three screws, the mid one still being attached to the shaft and the port and starboard ones lying on the ground by the ship. (Robert D. Turner collection)

John Williamson quickly ordered a replacement for *Queen Alexandra*. A second steamer of that name was ordered almost immediately from Denny's yard. She was of almost identical dimensions to the first steamer, and could be distinguished in that the bridge was a full deck higher than the promenade deck, and set back a few feet from the front of that deck. She had improved machinery, similar to that of *Duchess of Argyll*. Her speed was 21 1/2 knots and she could make 12 1/2 knots astern, a considerable improvement on her predecessor. She had the first steam steering engine in a Clyde steamer. She is seen here on trials with one of the lifeboats raised to a position halfway up the funnel.

Queen Alexandra's first public sailing was on 23 May 1912 from Greenock and Gourock to Campbeltown and she settled down on that service until the outbreak of war. (CRSC archive)

Queen Alexandra (1912) approaching Dunoon with *Lord of the Isles* in the distance.

Queen Alexandra (1912) at Lochranza here in around 1912 in a postcard view.

Queen Alexandra made ferry calls at Machrie, until the early 1920s, and at Pirnmill on the west coast of Arran. She is seen here at the latter place in an official postcard view.

Queen Alexandra (1912) arriving at Campbeltown in a Valentine's 'Artotype' postcard designed for the 'tartan tourist' market.

Queen Alexandra was requisitioned for war service in February 1915. She was used as a transport from the south of England to France and served until May 1919. On 9 May 1918 she rammed and sank a German U-boat. She re-entered civilian service on the Campbeltown route on 28 June of that year.

From 1920, following the re-entry into service of *King Edward*, until 1926. *Queen Alexandra* was on the Inveraray route, where she is seen here at Strachur.

Queen Alexandra at Inveraray in a postcard view. (CRSC Archive)

Passengers disembarking from *Queen Alexandra* at Inveraray. (CRSC Archive)

A Turbine Steamers handbill for 1924, showing *Queen Alexandra* and a map of the routes to Campbeltown and Inveraray. (Tom Lee collection)

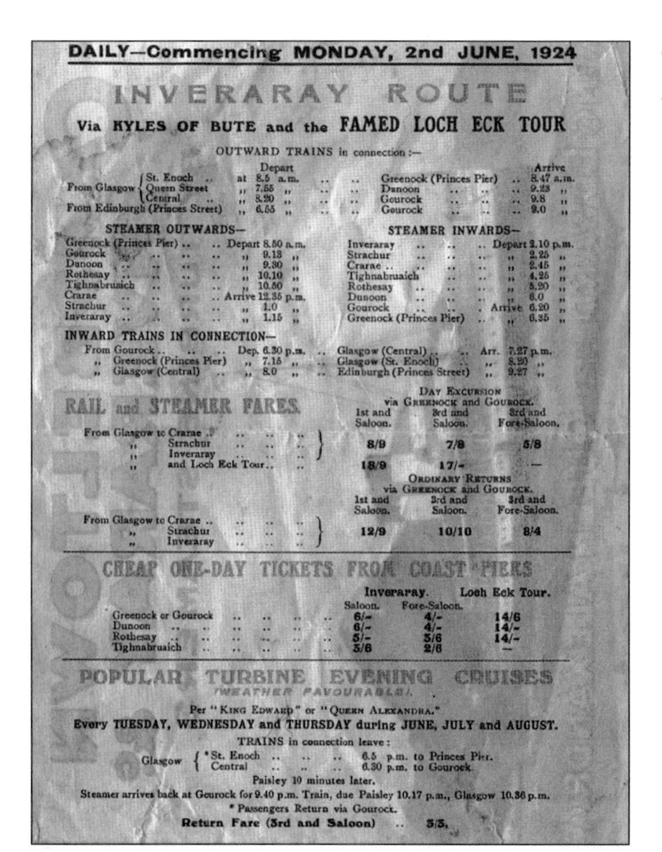

DAILY—Commencing MONDAY, 2nd JUNE, 1924

INVERARAY ROUTE

Via KYLES OF BUTE and the FAMED LOCH ECK TOUR

OUTWARD TRAINS in connection:—

		Depart		Arrive
From Glasgow	St. Enoch	at 8.5 a.m.	Greenock (Princes Pier)	8.47 a.m.
	Queen Street	,, 7.55 ,,	Dunoon	9.23 ,,
	Central	,, 8.20 ,,	Gourock	9.8 ,,
From Edinburgh (Princes Street)		,, 6.55 ,,	Gourock	9.0 ,,

STEAMER OUTWARDS—		STEAMER INWARDS—	
Greenock (Princes Pier)	Depart 8.50 a.m.	Inveraray	Depart 2.10 p.m.
Gourock	,, 9.13 ,,	Strachur	,, 2.25 ,,
Dunoon	,, 9.30 ,,	Crarae	,, 2.45 ,,
Rothesay	,, 10.10 ,,	Tighnabruaich	,, 4.25 ,,
Tighnabruaich	,, 10.50 ,,	Rothesay	,, 5.20 ,,
Crarae	Arrive 12.35 p.m.	Dunoon	,, 6.0 ,,
Strachur	,, 1.0 ,,	Gourock	Arrive 6.20 ,,
Inveraray	,, 1.15 ,,	Greenock (Princes Pier)	,, 6.35 ,,

INWARD TRAINS IN CONNECTION—

From Gourock	Dep. 6.30 p.m.	Glasgow (Central)	Arr. 7.27 p.m.
,, Greenock (Princes Pier)	,, 7.15 ,,	Glasgow (St. Enoch)	,, 8.20 ,,
,, Glasgow (Central)	,, 8.0 ,,	Edinburgh (Princes Street)	,, 9.27 ,,

RAIL and STEAMER FARES.

	Day Excursion via Greenock and Gourock. 1st and Saloon.	3rd and Saloon.	3rd and Fore-Saloon.
From Glasgow to Crarae / ,, Strachur / ,, Inveraray	8/9	7/8	5/8
,, and Loch Eck Tour	18/9	17/-	—

	Ordinary Returns via Greenock and Gourock. 1st and Saloon.	3rd and Saloon.	3rd and Fore-Saloon.
From Glasgow to Crarae / ,, Strachur / ,, Inveraray	12/9	10/10	8/4

CHEAP ONE-DAY TICKETS FROM COAST PIERS

	Inveraray. Saloon.	Inveraray. Fore-Saloon.	Loch Eck Tour.
Greenock or Gourock	6/-	4/-	14/6
Dunoon	6/-	4/-	14/-
Rothesay	5/-	3/6	14/-
Tighnabruaich	3/6	2/6	—

POPULAR TURBINE EVENING CRUISES
(WEATHER FAVOURABLE).

Per "King Edward" or "Queen Alexandra."

Every TUESDAY, WEDNESDAY and THURSDAY during JUNE, JULY and AUGUST.

TRAINS in connection leave:

Glasgow { *St. Enoch .. 6.5 p.m. to Princes Pier.
Central .. 6.30 p.m. to Gourock.

Paisley 10 minutes later.

Steamer arrives back at Gourock for 9.40 p.m. Train, due Paisley 10.17 p.m., Glasgow 10.36 p.m.

* Passengers Return via Gourock.

Return Fare (3rd and Saloon) .. 5/3.

The 1924 timetable for *Queen Alexandra's* sailings to Inveraray. (Tom Lee collection)

In 1927, following the advent of *King George V*, *Queen Alexandra* was moved back to the Campbeltown service. She is seen here off Greenock Esplanade in June 1928. (A. Ernest Glen collection)

A handbill for cruises to Rothesay illuminations and fireworks on 29 August 1930 by *Queen Alexandra* and *King George V*, with train connections from Glasgow. (CRSC Archive)

Fireworks and Illumination

— AT —

ROTHESAY

Friday, 29th August, 1930

TRAVEL via ST. ENOCH and PRINCES PIER for

TURBINE STEAMERS

"King George V."

— and —

"Queen Alexandra"

EXPRESS TRAINS in connection leave Glasgow (St. Enoch) at 6-0 and 6-20 p.m.

PAISLEY (Gilmour Street) at 6-10 and 6-18 p.m.

Return Fares, Rail and Steamer:

3rd and Saloon, - - 3/3

1st and Saloon, - - - - - 4/4

OBSERVE.—Passengers may travel per 5-44 p.m. Train St. Enoch to Princes Pier, due 6-34, and have their Tea in the Restaurant De Luxe on Board Turbine Steamer.

Full Tea, 3/-; One-Course Tea, 2/6

JOHN WILLIAMSON & CO., 308 Clyde Street, Glasgow, C.1

TURBINE STEAMERS LTD.

DAILY EXCURSION

— TO —

CAMPBELTOWN

and

Machrihanish & Southend Tours

in connection

Allowing about 2 hours at Campbeltown, 1 hour at Machrihanish, or ½ hour at Southend

Messrs. GORDON BROS.' BUS

Leaves WHITING BAY at 9.15 p.m.

DAILY for BRODICK

Where Passengers change to NORTH ARRAN MOTOR

For LOCHRANZA

in Connection with

T.S. "Queen Alexandra"

Due back Whiting Bay at 5.45 p.m.

RETURN DAY EXCURSION FARE (Bus and Steamer)

WHITING BAY to CAMPBELTOWN, : 7/-

Machrihanish Tour, 1/- extra Southend Tour, 2/- extra

TICKETS obtainable at GORDON BROS., Garage, Whiting Bay

John Williamson & Co., 308 Clyde Street, Glasgow, C.1.

Sam Lithgow, Printer, Glasgow.

A handbill for day trips to Campbeltown from Whiting Bay with bus connections to Lochranza. (CRSC Archive)

HEALTH & PLEASURE

GRAND HIGHLAND

Cabaret Cruise

wandering to the

THREE LOCHS

(Loch Fyne, Loch Ridden and Loch Striven)

By the Clyde's Largest Turbine Steamer

"Queen Alexandra"

On Saturday 12th August

Leaving GOUROCK 6.10. DUNOON 6.30
LARGS 7.20. ROTHESAY 7.50

MUSIC, DANCING and COMMUNITY SINGING

NOVELTIES
Lady finding the LORD OF THE ISLES
Gentleman finding MARY OF ARGYLL
(Valuable Prizes)

Cruise Fare . . . 2/-

Juveniles H.P. It's an H.P. Cruise

Queen Alexandra did her fair share of evening cruises, like the one advertised here to the Three Lochs on Saturday 12 August 1933. (CRSC Archive)

B. B. C.

: This is a Bright and Breezy Cruise :

On Sunday, 15th July

TO

ARROCHAR

(LOCH LONG)

By Magnificent Steamer

"Queen Alexandra"

Come and view the magnificent scenery of the beautiful hills of Bute and Cowal coast, also sailing through the placid waters of Loch Goil and Loch Long

Keppel - 6.20 Largs - 7.0
Fairlie - 6.40[A] Rothesay 7.30
Dunoon - 8.0[B]

[A] Fairlie passengers land at Largs on return journey
[B] Dunoon passengers return via Largs, Keppel and Rothesay
Young's Bus in connection to Kilbirnie, Lochwinnoch, Paisley, and Glasgow.

Fare, 2/-; Juveniles, 1/-

SAM LITHGOW, Printer Glasgow

A handbill for a BBC (Bright and Breezy Cruise) by *Queen Alexandra* to Arrochar on Sunday 15 July 1934, from Keppel, Fairlie, Largs, Rothesay and Dunoon. It will be seen that she started picking up passengers for the evening cruise during her return journey from Campbeltown.

In 1932, *Queen Alexandra's* upper deck was enclosed to give her a more modern appearance. There was, however, no saloon inside this, just bare deck space.

Queen Alexandra approaching Fairlie with thick black smoke billowing from her funnels, post-1932.

Queen Alexandra arriving at Campbeltown between 1932 and 1935 in a postcard view, which was still on sale there in the late 1960s. Following the sale of Turbine Steamers Ltd to David Macbrayne Ltd on 3 December 1935 she briefly, whilst in winter lay-up, had her funnels painted in Macbrayne red.

By the following summer, however, she had had a third, dummy, funnel added and had been renamed *St Columba*. She was placed on the Ardrishaig mail service, which she maintained until her withdrawal and scrapping after the 1958 summer season. For the remainder of her history see *MacBrayne Steamers*.

King George V was the fourth and final turbine to be built for Turbine Steamers Ltd. She came, like the previous three, from the yard of William Denny at Dumbarton and is seen here shortly after her launch on 29 April 1926.

King George V was built with revolutionary high-pressure turbines. She had twin propeller shafts rather than the three of previous turbines. One of the shafts had four turbines, working on a quadruple-expansion basis, and the other had three turbines, working as a triple-expansion set. These turbines were geared unlike the earlier turbine steamers, which were direct drive. She is seen here fitting out at Dumbarton under the famous 247ft high Dumbarton Rock.

King George V had the first enclosed promenade deck on a Clyde steamer and the first observation saloon on that deck. She also had her dining saloon on the main deck aft, whereas on previous Clyde steamers it had been on the lower deck aft. She is seen here on trials in August 1926. She entered service on 8 September of that year.

A well-filled *King George V* in a card captioned 'T. S. *King George V* on a cruise round Ailsa Craig'. She operated a total of six such special cruises to mark the opening of the Williamson-Buchanan season on Saturdays in May of 1927, 1930 and 1934. These were otherwise undertaken by *Queen Alexandra*.

At the start of her career *King George V* was advertised as the 'New Super Turbine'. She is illustrated here on the cover of the Turbine Steamers Timetable for 1930. (G.E. Langmuir collection, Mitchell Library)

An advertisement for the Round Ailsa Craig cruise in 1934. (CRSC Archive)

King George V approaching Lochranza prior to 1929. (CRSC)

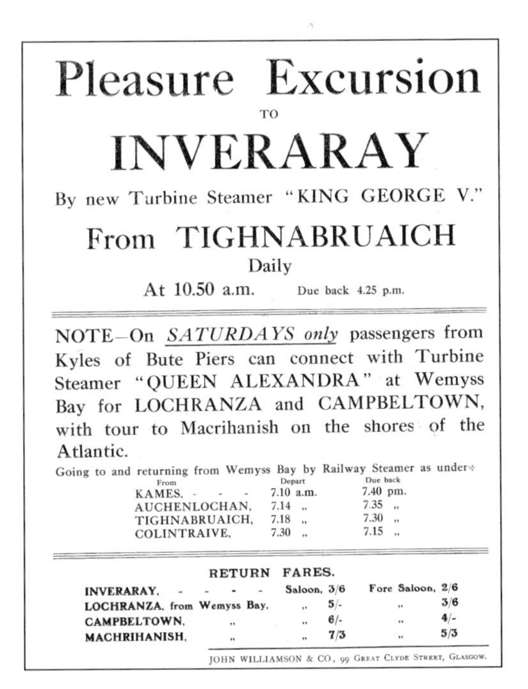

Above left: A handbill for cruises by *King George V* from Tighnabruaich to Inveraray and also for Saturday connections from Kames, Auchenlochan, Tighnabruaich and Colintraive to connect with *Queen Alexandra* for Lochranza and Campbeltown. (CRSC Archive). *Above right:* Another handbill for cruises from Tighnabruaich to Inveraray and the single journey back to Princes Pier. The Loch Eck tour was carried out by bus from Strachur to Dunoon following the withdrawal of *Fairy Queen* on Loch Eck in 1926. (CRSC Archive)

King George V mainly served Inveraray, replacing *King Edward* on that route, with occasional forays to Campbeltown and very occasional downriver sailings. On 29 September 1927 she was sailing to winter lay-up at Irvine when she suffered a steam tube in the boiler, which caused an explosion that blew the furnace doors off and resulted in the death of two firemen. She had no wireless and was in danger of drifting onto the beach but she was spotted by the coaster *Prase*, which held her off until a tug came to tow her into Irvine about three hours later. (A. Ernest Glen)

In 1929 *King George V* was re-boilered and the lifeboats were moved to the after end of the upper deck. At the same time her funnels received navy tops. She is seen here in that condition at Strachur.

Above: King George V at Gourock in 1926. *Below: King George V* departing Dunoon. (CRSC Archive)

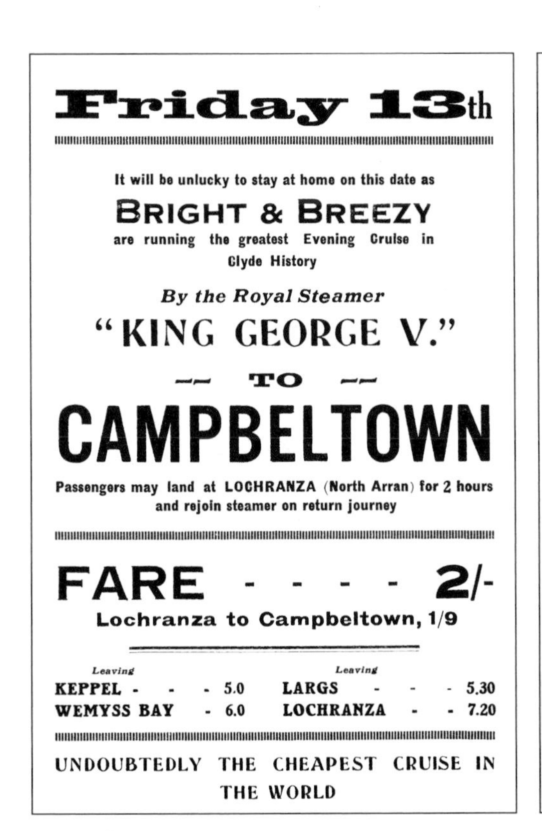

Friday 13th

It will be unlucky to stay at home on this date as

BRIGHT & BREEZY

are running the greatest Evening Cruise in Clyde History

By the Royal Steamer

"KING GEORGE V."

TO

CAMPBELTOWN

Passengers may land at LOCHRANZA (North Arran) for 2 hours and rejoin steamer on return journey

FARE - - - - 2/-

Lochranza to Campbeltown, 1/9

Leaving		Leaving	
KEPPEL - - -	5.0	LARGS - - -	5.30
WEMYSS BAY -	6.0	LOCHRANZA - -	7.20

UNDOUBTEDLY THE CHEAPEST CRUISE IN THE WORLD

SPECIAL

EVENING CRUISES

(WEATHER FAVOURABLE)

BY NEW TURBINE STEAMER

"King George V."

On Saturday, 2nd July

To CORRIE (Arran)

From	PRINCES PIER - -	6-30
,,	DUNOON - - -	6-50
,,	ROTHESAY - - -	7-30

On Wednesday, 6th July

To BRODICK BAY

From	GOUROCK - - -	6-15
,,	PRINCES PIER - -	6-30
,,	DUNOON - - -	6-50
,,	ROTHESAY - - -	7-25

MUSIC ON BOARD

Cruise Fare, 2/-

JOHN WILLIAMSON & Co., 99 Great Clyde Street, Glasgow, C.1.

Above left: On Friday 13 July 1934, *King George V* offered an evening cruise to Campbeltown as the remarkably low fare of 2*s* (10p) – as it says here 'undoubtedly the cheapest cruise in the world'. (CRSC Archive). *Above right:* More common destinations for evening cruises were Corrie and Brodick Bay, as featured in this handbill from July 1932. (CRSC Archive)

King George V off Tighnabruaich in her final season as a White Funnel steamer. In February of that year she was fitted with a third set of boilers and one of the turbines from the set of four was removed. At that time she received a set of thicker funnels as seen here.

On 3 October 1935 *King George V* was taken over by David MacBrayne Ltd and the following summer was placed on the service from Oban to Staffa and Iona, which she made her own until withdrawn after the 1974 season. For the remainder of her history see *MacBrayne Steamers*. (Douglas Brown collection)

The final White Funnel turbine, *Queen Mary*, was launched on 30 March 1933 at the Dumbarton yard of William Denny & Bros. Ltd. She was built for the downriver sailings and was thus owned by Williamson-Buchanan Steamers Ltd, and not Turbine Steamers Ltd. She had the largest passenger capacity, at over 2,000, of any Clyde steamer of that time. She reverted to direct drive turbines rather than the geared turbines that had been fitted in *King George V*.

Queen Mary, seen here in an 'on board' postcard (actually a view of her leaving for her trials), entered service on 20 May 1933 and soon established herself on the 10:00 cruise to Rothesay and the Arran coast.

The destination of *Queen Mary's* afternoon cruise to the Arran coast varied. This undated handbill from 1933 advertises one of these from Largs and Keppel round Inchmarnock. She sailed on Mondays and Wednesdays to Skipness, on Tuesdays to Lamlash, on Thursdays to Brodick (non-landing) and on Saturdays to the Cock of Arran.

Queen Mary passing Anderston Quay in 1933. The takeover of Williamson-Buchanan by the LMSR on 1 October 1935 made no real difference to her sailings.

On 10 April 1935, Williamson-Buchanan applied to have the name of *Queen Mary* changed to *Queen Mary II*, to free the name for the new Cunarder.

Kylemore passing No.534, the future Cunard Liner *Queen Mary*, building at John Brown's yard at Clydebank. (C. & J. McCutcheon collection)

SEPTEMBER, 1934

WILLIAMSON-BUCHANAN STEAMERS, LTD.

GLASGOW and THE COAST

(Viewing the New Cunarder No. 534 at Clydebank)

ALL-THE-WAY DAILY SAILINGS

as under :—

from

GLASGOW (Bridge Wharf, South Side), calling at Govan & Renfrew

By the Magnificent Steamers

New Turbine "QUEEN MARY,"
Turbine "KING EDWARD,"
P.S "EAGLE," "QUEEN EMPRESS"
and "KYLEMORE"

f "EAGLE" - - - - - - - - 10.0 a.m.
For Kirn, Dunoon, Innellan and Rothesay.

T.S. "KING EDWARD" (or other Steamer) - 11.0 a.m.
For Princes Pier, Kirn, Dunoon, Innellan, Rothesay and Cruise.

"KYLEMORE" - - - - - - - - 1.30 p.m.
For Princes Pier, Kirn, Dunoon, Innellan and Rothesay.

Returning from
ROTHESAY Daily at 8.15 a.m., *d*2.45, 4.40, and *6.15 p.m.
DUNOON Daily at 9.10 a.m., *d*3.30, 5.25, and *6.50 p.m.
f Ceases after 15th September. * Saturdays only except 29th.
d Ceases after 15th September and except 4th, 6th, 8th, and 10th

Subject to Alterations, for which see Glasgow Newspapers, or apply
JOHN WILLIAMSON & CO., 308 Clyde Street, Glasgow, C.1

The September 1934 leaflet for Williamson-Buchanan's sailings from Glasgow Bridge Wharf. Note the comment 'Viewing the New Cunarder No.534 at Clydebank'.

WILLIAMSON-BUCHANAN STEAMERS, LTD.

TIME-TABLE, from 3rd Sept. till 30th Sept., 1934

SPECIAL SAILINGS on 4th, 6th, 10th and 17th September

From Glasgow Bridge Wharf (S.S.) at 10 a.m., Govan 10-10, Renfrew 10-30 a.m.

By New Turbine Steamer "QUEEN MARY"

To DUNOON, ROTHESAY, LARGS, KEPPEL, and CRUISES AS UNDER.

4th	HOLY ISLE	10th	LOCHRANZA
6th	SKIPNESS	17th	SKIPNESS

Returning from Keppel 4-20 p.m., Largs 4-40 p.m., Rothesay 5-30 p.m., Dunoon 6 p.m.

GLASGOW TO THE COAST

Viewing the New Cunarder No. 534 at Clydebank.

FROM BRIDGE WHARF (South Side)

	Daily E	Daily	Daily Ex Sats.	Saturdays only except 29th	Saturdays, only
Glasgow (Bridge Wharf) Stmr. dep.	10.0 a.m.	11.0 a.m.	1.30 p.m.	1.45 p.m.	c1.45 p.m.
Govan	10.10 a.m.	11.10 a.m.	1.40 p.m.	1.55 p.m.	c1.55 p.m.
Renfrew	10.30 a.m.	11.30 a.m.	2.0 p.m.	2.15 p.m.	c2.15 p.m.
St. Enoch ... ... Train dep.	—	b11.28 a.m.	—	—	—
Central ... ... Train dep.	—	—	—	—	3.0 p.m.
Princes Pier	—	12.50 p.m.	3.20 p.m.	—	3.40 p.m.
Gourock	—	—	—	—	4.0 p.m.
Kirn ... ... arr.	12.10 p.m.	1.15 p.m.	3.50 p.m.	—	4.20 p.m.
Dunoon ... ... ,,	12.15 p.m.	1.25 p.m.	4.0 p.m.	3.55 p.m.	4.30 p.m.
Innellan ... ... ,,	12.40 p.m.	1.45 p.m.	4.30 p.m.	—	5.0 p.m.
Rothesay ... ... ,,	1.5 p.m.	2.10 p.m.	5.5 p.m.	4.35 p.m.	5.30 p.m.
Port-Bannatyne ... ... ,,	—	n2.35 p.m. Thence Cruise	—	— Thence Cruise	—

E Ceases after 15th September, and except 8th. b Saturdays 12.9 p.m. c 29th September only.
n Saturdays only till 15th September, then Mons., Weds., Thurs. and Sats.

FOR SUNDAY SAILINGS SEE OPPOSITE PAGE.

FROM THE COAST

Viewing the New Cunarder No· 534 at Clydebank.

	Daily	Daily A	Daily	Saturdays only Except 29th
Port-Bannatyne	—	—	n4.15 p.m.	—
Rothesay	8.15 a.m.	2.45 p.m.	4.40 p.m.	6.15 p.m.
Innellan	8.35 a.m.	3.5 p.m.	5.0 p.m.	—
Dunoon	9.10 a.m.	3.30 p.m.	5.25 p.m.	6.50 p.m.
Kirn	9.20 a.m.	3.35 p.m.	5.30 p.m.	—
Princes Pier	9.50 a.m.	—	6.0 p.m.	—
Renfrew	11.20 a.m.	5.30 p.m.	7.20 p.m.	8.45 p.m.
Govan	11.40 a.m.	5.50 p.m.	7.40 p.m.	9.5 p.m.
Glasgow (Bridge Wharf, South Side)	11.50 a.m.	6.0 p.m.	7.50 p.m.	9.15 p.m

n Saturdays only till 15th September, then Mons., Weds., Thurs. and Sats.
A Ceases after 15th September, and except 4th, 6th, and 10th, September

For Special Sailings on 22nd and 24th Sept., See Glasgow Newspapers

FARES FROM GLASGOW

	SINGLE 1st Cabin	SINGLE 2nd Cabin	RETURN 1st Cabin	RETURN 2nd Cabin
DUNOON	2/-	1/3	3/-	2/-
ROTHESAY	2/6	1/9	3/6	2/6
DAY'S SAIL at 11 a.m. ...			4/6	3/6
Do. with Dinner and Plain Tea			8/6	—
Do. do. do. High Tea			9/6	—
DAY'S SAIL at 10 a.m. ...			5/-	4/-
Do. do. with Dinner and High Tea			10/-	9/-
AFTERNOON SAIL, DUNOON, with High Tea			5/-	—
SATURDAY AFTERNOON EXCURSION, KYLES CRUISE			4/-	3/-
Do. do. do. DUNOON, with High Tea			5/-	—
Do. do. do. ROTHESAY, do.			5/6	—
Do. do. do. KYLES CRUISE do.			6/-	—

DAILY AFTERNOON EXCURSION

(Viewing the NEW CUNARDER)

By Steamer "KYLEMORE"

From GLASGOW, Bridge Wharf (South Side) at **1.30** p.m.

(Saturdays at **1.45** p.m.—See below)

TO DUNOON

Returning from DUNOON by T.S. "King Edward" (or other Steamer) at **5.25** p.m.

Due back GLASGOW at **7.50** p.m.

Sail, 3/- or 2/- ; with High Tea, 5/-

DAILY AFTERNOON CRUISES

FROM COAST

By T.S. "KING EDWARD" or P.S. "EAGLE"

From GREENOCK (Princes Pier), **12.50** p.m., DUNOON, **1.25** p.m., ROTHESAY, **2.25** p.m.

Mons. and Thurs. ...	LOCH STRIVEN
Tues. and Fris.	ROUND CUMBRAES
Weds., Sats. and Suns.	KYLES OF BUTE

Calling at PORT-BANNATYNE on Saturdays till 15th, then Mondays, Wednesdays, Thursdays and Saturdays.

Cruise Fares from	Weekdays	Sundays
GREENOCK	2/6 or 2/-	3/3 or 2/6
DUNOON	1/6 —	2/6 —
ROTHESAY	1/- —	1/6 or 1/-

Delightful SATURDAY AFTERNOON EXCURSIONS

Except 29th September

From GLASGOW, Bridge Wharf (South Side), at 1.45 p.m., calling at Govan and Renfrew.

Direct to DUNOON. and ROTHESAY, thence Cruise through the Far-famed KYLES OF BUTE to LOCH RIDDEN, by new Turbine "QUEEN MARY"

T.S. "KING EDWARD" on 22nd September.

Turbine Steamer returns from **Rothesay at 6.15** p.m., **Dunoon 6.50** p.m., for Renfrew, Govan and Glasgow.

. For Fares see opposite page.

SUNDAY PLEASURE SAILS

From GLASGOW, Bridge Wharf (South Side)

To DUNOON, ROTHESAY, LARGS, KEPPEL and LOCHGOILHEAD Cruises to KYLES OF BUTE ARRAN, etc.

OUTWARDS.

	A a.m.	a.m.	B p.m.
GLASGOW, Bridge Wharf dep.	10 30	11 0	2 15
GOVAN ,,	...	11 10	2 25
BOWLING ,,	...	12 0n	...
PRINCES PIER ,,	...	12 45p	...
DUNOON arr.	12 35p	1 20	4 25
INNELLAN ,,	...	1 40	...
ROTHESAY ,,	1 25	2 5	...
LARGS ,,	2 10	...	...
KEPPEL ,,	2 20	...	...
LOCHGOILHEAD ,,	...	...	5 20

INWARDS.

	p.m.	A p.m.	B p.m.
LOCHGOILHEAD dep.	...	...	6 0
KEPPEL ,,	...	4 25	...
LARGS ,,	...	4 35	...
ROTHESAY ,,	4 40	5 30	...
INNELLAN ,,	5 0	...	...
DUNOON ,,	5 25	6 0	7 [illegible]5
PRINCES PIER arr.	6 0	...	...
BOWLING ,,	6 50	...	...
GOVAN ,,	7 40	8 10	9 10
GLASGOW, Bridge Wharf ,,	7 50	8 20	9 20

A—2nd September only. B—Except 30th Sept.

Turbine Steamer "QUEEN MARY" from **Glasgow** at **10.30** a.m. on 2nd Sept. only, leaves **ROTHESAY** at **1.35** p.m. for Cruise to Arran, etc., *via* Largs and Keppel.

T.S. "QUEEN MARY" (P.S. "EAGLE" on 2nd) from **Glasgow** at **11** a.m. will cruise each Sunday to Kyles of Bute, leaving **ROTHESAY** at **2.25** p.m.

T.S. "KING EDWARD" from **Glasgow** at **2.15** p.m. to Dunoon and Lochgoilhead (time on shore)

SUNDAY RETURN FARES

	1st Cab.	2nd Cab.	With Dinner and Plain Tea	With Dinner and High Tea
Glasgow to Dunoon	3/-	2/6	—	—
Glasgow to Rothesay Largs or Keppel...	3/6	3/-	8/-	9/-
Glasgow and Cruise to Arran, Round Bute, etc. ...	5/-	4/-	9/6	10/6
Glasgow and Cruise to Kyles of Bute...	4/6	3/6	9/-	10/-

CHEAP AFTERNOON FARES

	1st Cab.	2nd Cab.	With High Tea
Glasgow to Dunoon ...	3/-	2/-	5/-
Glasgow to Lochgoilhead ...	3/6	2/6	5/6

The Williamson-Buchanan timetable for September 1934. Note that by this stage of the season, *Queen Mary* only offered occasional trips to the Arran coast. She often offered long-distance cruises from Gourock, for example to Campbeltown via the Kyles or Round the Lochs in the Septembers of her first three seasons.

The war years saw *Queen Mary II* remain on the Clyde, although there were no Bridge Wharf sailings. She was the mainstay of the Gourock to Dunoon run and was also used tendering to troopships at the Tail of the Bank. On 27 February 1943 ownership was transferred to the Caledonian Steam Packet Co. Ltd. She is seen here, bottom left, as she ran in 1945 with CSP yellow and black funnels but still with a wartime grey hull.

During the war years, *Queen Mary II* had received a crosstrees on her mast. In 1946 she returned to the 10:00 sailing from Bridge Wharf. Renfrew calls did not resume after the war and outward Govan calls were halted after the 1946 season. The inbound calls at Govan ceased after 1953.

In 1948, in common with the remainder of the Clyde steamers, *Queen Mary II* received a wheelhouse. It was said that this was at the instigation of the National Union of Railwaymen. It was not until 1951 that the canvas dodgers on the bridge wings were replaced by wooden ones.

1952 saw *Queen Mary II* moved to the 11:00 sailing from Bridge Wharf to Tighnabruaich, following the withdrawal of *King Edward*. In 1954 she was fitted with a mainmast to comply with new lighting regulations. (CRSC)

Above: In 1957 *Queen Mary II* was reboilered at Barclay Curle's and fitted with a single, wider funnel. She is seen here in a postcard view leaving Glasgow Bridge Wharf.

Opposite above: *Queen Mary II* passing Dumbarton Rock between 1957 and 1964.

Opposite middle: A postcard view of *Queen Mary II* arriving at Rothesay in the same period.

Opposite below: *Queen Mary II* at Tighnabruaich, also in her 1957-1964 condition.

In 1965 *Queen Mary II*, seen here off Greenock Great Harbour from the steamer returning from the Friday up-river cruise, in common with the remainder of the CSP fleet, received a lion on each side of her funnel and had her hull painted in Monastral Blue.

Following the withdrawal of *Duchess of Montrose* and *Jeanie Deans* at the end of the 1964 season, from 1965 *Queen Mary II* did not run from Bridge Wharf in Saturdays, being employed on railway connection work from Gourock and Wemyss Bay. From 1967 her Sunday cruise was altered to a round Bute cruise. She is seen here in the 1964-64 winter with newly applied lions on her funnels, at Greenock with *Duchess of Hamilton* and *Duchess of Montrose*.

On 23 September 1967 the Clyde River Steamer Club chartered *Queen Mary II* for a cruise which included a landing at Corrie by ferry, seen here. (CRSC)

Queen Mary II off Largs in 1968.

A stern view of *Queen Mary II* leaving Largs in 1968.

In 1969 *Queen Mary II's* masts had been shortened to pass below the Kingston Bridge, although the steamer never ventured that far up the Clyde after the bridge was completed. This was the last season that Bridge Wharf was used and charter sailings from the city moved to Princes Dock, where *Queen Mary II* is seen with *Duchess of Hamilton* in 1970. (CRSC)

In 1970 a black hull replaced the Monastral blue one. In the same year *Queen Mary II*, seen here arriving at Keppel Pier on 5 September of that year, effectively replaced *Caledonia*, sailing on Mondays to Arran via the Kyles and from Tuesdays to Fridays and Sundays Round Bute. On Saturday afternoons she did a cruise to Tarbert Bay.

After the 1971 season, Lochranza, Fairlie and Keppel piers were closed and the Campbeltown sailings were routed via Brodick. *Queen Mary II* is seen at Keppel on 5 September 1970 on the occasion of a Clyde Steamer Club Three Steamers day, which included sails on *Queen Mary II*, *Duchess of Hamilton* and *Waverley*.

Prior to the 1971 season, *Queen Mary II* had a major refurbishment of her passenger accommodation. Her main restaurant was converted to a cafeteria and the Queens Restaurant was created in her former bar in the lower deck, with the bar moved to the former cafeteria. She is seen here at Rothesay.

From 1971, following the withdrawal of *Duchess of Hamilton*, *Queen Mary II* was assigned to the longer distance excursions to Inveraray on Tuesdays; Lochranza and Campbeltown on Mondays, Thursdays, Saturdays and Sundays; Brodick and Pladda via the Kyles on Wednesdays; and Brodick and Pladda via Keppel on Fridays. She is seen here behind the pier buildings at Campbeltown with *Sound of Islay*, which was then on a service to Red Bay in Northern Ireland at the inside berth.

In 1973 *Queen Mary II* appeared in the new Caledonian MacBrayne livery with a red black-topped funnel and the lion inside a yellow circle. She is seen here at Campbeltown in 1976.

In 1974, following the withdrawal of *Waverley*, *Queen Mary II* assumed the mantle of the sole surviving Clyde excursion steamer. She was moved to shorter cruises – Round Bute or Round the Lochs – with a Saturday afternoon jaunt to Tighnabruaich, and is seen here off Dunoon. (Robin B. Boyd)

In 1976 *Queen Mary II* was named *Queen Mary* again, the famous Cunarder having been out of service then for some nine years. She is seen here arriving at Gourock in 1977.

Queen Mary retained to the end this window in the captain's cabin below the bridge, engraved with the words 'Queen Mary Glasgow' surrounding the star and crescent Williamson house-flag, the same flag which had been used for Alexander Williamson's Turkish Fleet a century and more before.

In 1976 and 1977 Caledonian MacBrayne marketed *Queen Mary* as 'Britain's finest pleasure steamer'. This title had been given to her by Williamson-Buchanan in her early seasons.

'Finished with engines' – *Queen Mary* in Greenock's East India Harbour in spring 1978. Various abortive plans were mooted for her preservation and she was eventually sold for use on the Thames as a static bar-restaurant. She left Greenock under tow on 29 January 1981 and, after a further sale to Bass Charrington, was opened, moored on the Thames Embankment, in 1989.

Queen Mary was fitted with two new funnels; they were somewhat narrower than the original ones, which have appeared in various colour schemes since 1989. Her turbines have been removed and her passenger accommodation totally transformed. She is now welded to a riverbank pontoon. Still, she survives – the last remnant of the White Funnel Fleet.